HOW EXAMS *REALLY* WORK

DA

373.126

Also available from Cassell:

S. Cowley: *Starting Teaching*

C. Cullingford (ed.): *Assessment Versus Evaluation*

A. Gold: *Head of Department*

D. Hamilton: *Passing Exams*

L. Nyatanga, Dawn Forman and Jane Fox: *Good Practice in the Accreditation of Prior Learning*

C. Taylor Fitz-Gibbon: *Monitoring Education*

How Exams *Really* Work

The Cassell Guide to GCSEs, AS and A Levels

J. G. Lloyd

CASSELL

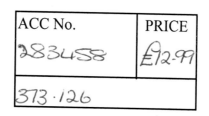
Cassell

Wellington House
125 Strand
London WC2R 0BB

370 Lexington Avenue
New York
NY 10017–6550

© J. G. Lloyd 1999

First published 1999

British Library Cataloguing-in-Publication Data
A catalogue record for this book is available from the British Library.

ISBN   0-304-70690-6

Typeset by Kenneth Burnley, Wirral, Cheshire.
Printed and bound in Great Britain by Redwood Books, Trowbridge, Wiltshire.

Contents

Abbreviations and Acronyms

SEC   Secondary Examinations Council
SEAC   School Examinations and Assessment Council
SCAA   School Curriculum and Assessment Authority
QCA   Qualifications and Curriculum Authority
AEB   Associated Examining Board
INSET   in-service training
EDI   electronic data interchange
MEI   Mathematics in Education and Industry
SMP   School Mathematics Project
UMS   Uniform Mark Scale
GAC   Grading Advisory Committee
OCSEB   Oxford and Cambridge Schools Examination Board
IAASE   Independent Appeals Authority for School Examinations
OFSTED   Office for Standards in Education
SPAG   spelling, punctuation and grammar
SUJB   Southern Universities Joint Board
MEG   Midland Examining Group
UCLES   University of Cambridge Local Examinations Syndicate
UODLE   University of Oxford Delegacy of Local Examinations
SEG   Southern Examining Group
OCEAC   Oxford and Cambridge Examinations and Assessment Council

BTEC	Business Technician Education Council
RSA	Royal Society of Arts
EDEXCEL	(the acronym of the London/BTEC Board)
OCR	Oxford, Cambridge and RSA
NEAB	Northern Examinations and Assessment Board
AQA	Assessment and Qualifications Alliance
NVQ	National Vocational Qualification
GNVQ	General National Vocational Qualification
DfEE	Department for Education and Employment

Introduction

Examining Boards are the unknown element in British education. Few people in the country have never actually taken an examination. Few have not been involved with friends or relatives taking examinations. Yet how much is known about the process? The candidate enters the examination room and is presented with a question paper. Two hours later, or after whatever time the length of the examination dictates, the script is handed in. Perhaps six or eight weeks later a result is received. But who set the question paper? How was its standard of difficulty assured? Who marked the script? Who decided what result the consequent mark deserved, and by what criteria? (And why did it take so long to produce the result?)

Every summer when GCSE and A-Level results are published the press (and usually politicians too) have much to say about standards. Every press pundit, every bar-room pundit, 'knows' that standards have fallen (or not). But how do they, how might they know? What criteria would they use?

No doubt too there is much mythology bandied about among parents, or even in schools which ought to know better, at examination time: 'Your son's result was disappointing, but all you have to do is appeal and the grade will be put up.' Will it? 'Get a doctor to certify that your daughter is dyslexic and the Board will give her the benefit of the doubt.' Is that true? 'Make sure that your son is entered for the coursework option. It's easier than the alternative.' Is it really? 'We hadn't been taught what was on the question paper. Our teacher hadn't covered it. But if we write to the Board they'll make an allowance for it.' Will they?

This book attempts to answer these questions and many more. It is written for anyone concerned about the public examinations for GCSE, AS and A Level, whether as educational experts, teachers or parents. I write it with the experience of having been an assistant examiner from the late '60s, a chief examiner for two separate Boards from the early '70s until 1984, and a senior officer of an Examination Board from 1984 until 1997. During that time I was involved with implementing the introduction of GCSE and in various stages of revision of syllabuses at both levels. I have served on committees dealing with administration policy, syllabus approval, the writing of criteria for examinations in general, the examination timetable, handicapped candidates, malpractice, finalizing question papers, grading results and dealing with appeals. These committees have not only been within the Board for which I worked but also at inter-Board level and in dealings with the regulatory authority, first SEC, then SEAC, later SCAA, and now transformed into QCA. My specialism is in Classics, but I have served as Subject Officer for a range of subjects on the Arts and Languages side at both GCSE and A Level. This has involved close working with the examiners and much meeting with, corresponding with, and talking on the telephone to teachers. I have become very aware of the realities and problems involved in running and sitting examinations, and know that they are about real candidates whose difficulties may not fit neatly into preconceived policies and procedures.

I hope that this book will promote public understanding of school examinations by explaining what they are and can do (and what they are not and cannot do), and will be of real help to all involved with them, but especially to candidates, parents and teachers.

NOTE

Website

The examinations system is constantly in a state of flux. Updated information on the system is provided on the web page for this book, available through www.cassell-prof.co.uk. This site also provides links to examination board websites.

Chapter 1

What Is an Examining Board?

A COMMERCIAL VENTURE

An Examining Board is a commercial venture. This means that it is susceptible to bankruptcy and take-over. In recent years the latter has happened a number of times, and the former probably would have happened if a take-over had not intervened. The very recent reduction of the Examining Boards to three large operations or partnerships has made the collapse of any of the surviving three very unlikely, but it remains a theoretical possibility.

An Examining Board's main source of income is the entry fees paid by the candidates whom it examines. It also receives investment income earned partly on invested reserves and partly on investment between the entry fees being paid in February and the money going out to the examiners in August: an Examining Board delights in high interest rates over those six months! Some Boards succeeded in establishing examination services overseas, and these have had both the volume of business and the accumulated reserves to be secure. Others, with a small share of the UK market only, survived by a hair's breadth for many years, and were the ones which had to allow themselves to be swallowed up into the newly formed partnerships.

For these reasons Examining Boards compete with one another. First and foremost they compete in their entry fees. It is a matter of astonishment to the general public, and to many teachers also, when they realize that Examining Boards charge different entry fees from each other. It is even more of an astonishment when they realize that in cases where two or more Boards share a common syllabus, now admittedly very rare but until a few years ago quite common, the candidate would pay the fee set by the Board through which the entry is made. At the extreme a school could have saved £4 per candidate by switching its entry from the dearest to the cheapest Board. The candidate would have studied the same syllabus, sat the same examination paper, and been marked and graded by the same examining team. We are accustomed to finding branded goods carrying different prices in different supermarkets; it seems wrong that Examining Boards should behave like supermarkets, but basically they do.

In one respect, of course, Examining Boards cannot compete, namely in the grades which they award. If you buy a bag of apples from the greengrocer and one is rotten you will justifiably take it back and demand a perfect one in its place. If you take an examination and the grade awarded is a low one, or even a failure, you cannot demand a grade A replacement. The Board's responsibility to the candidate, and the product for which the candidate pays, is the correct result, whatever that turns out to be. Yet in the present age of school league tables, schools will do anything in their power to identify a Board or syllabus in which they believe they will obtain better results. A mythology grows and spreads that one Board is difficult, another easy, and the Boards find their entries (customers) moving accordingly.

This feeling on the part of schools is not new. When I took up my first teaching post in 1959 my headmaster said 'Of course we take the Oxford and Cambridge Board here', in tones indicating that that Board offered the highest quality and standards, and that any other was inferior. On the other hand I soon discovered that candidates who failed O Level, especially in the key subjects of English and Mathematics, were likely to be entered for their re-sit with another Board deemed to be easier. It is a gross calumny to my friends at the Associated Examining Board (commonly known as the AEB) that in some schools they used to be called the Awfully Easy Board. I am sure that this was not justified. The results did not seem to bear it out, but such mythologies become deeply rooted and still prevail to some extent.

Apart from entry fees, Examining Boards are having to learn to compete both in the services which they provide and in the image which they project. The former can only be good for the candidates and for the teachers who prepare them. Major developments have been in the provision of in-service training (INSET) and the publication of mark-schemes. There is also an effective and widely used result enquiry and appeals service. The old secrecy has gone. Looking back it seems remarkable that thirty or forty years ago a syllabus might have been no more than a page long, that for an idea of what the question paper would be like schools were dependent upon inherited wisdom derived from the experience of previous years, and that scripts were written and posted off for the results to appear six weeks later with no after-sales service available. Incidentally, I wonder how far this may still be true of the examinations of the professional bodies – accountants, bankers, lawyers, engineers etc. On the one occasion in my own career when I was formally approached for consultation by a representative of such a body (which I had better not identify!) it was abundantly clear that such was very much the case, although their decision to seek advice was a sign that they had realized the dangers and were keen to put them right.

Nowadays a syllabus spells out its aims, objectives and assessment criteria. Specimen papers are provided, teachers attend training meetings. All aspects of the examination are open to enquiry and appeal. It is true that much of this has been imposed on the Boards by the quality control bodies which supervise them, but it is equally true that they have pushed ahead with it, especially in the provision of training, as a means of competing with each other.

The Boards' competition for image makes a fascinating study. Look at their syllabus booklets, question papers and stationery of 30 years ago and look at them now. Designer logos, multi-coloured covers, user-friendly layout and typefaces, derived from the professional advice of design consultants and marketing specialists, have all appeared. They issue information leaflets or news-sheets regularly on glossy paper with colour printing and photographs. They all know, or think they know, that they have to do it. They have their own dedicated publicity and marketing departments. Chief Executives have to decide what they can afford to spend – with an impact on the entry fees – while knowing that they cannot afford not to spend considerable sums. Mailshots go to all centres, not just to those on a Board's registered list. As private individuals we all receive any amount of 'junk mail'. We know that it affects the price of the product it offers, but we can ignore it if we wish and need feel little concern if the business fails. But it seems quite wrong that an integral part of the education service should behave in this way, and should channel part of the candidates' entry fees into blatant commercial marketing.

EXAMINATION FEES

One aspect of commercial practice which Boards have not yet felt able to adopt is to price the syllabuses differently, each at true cost. We should be surprised if every item in a supermarket bore the same price, but we expect every A-Level syllabus, be it English, Physics or Russian, to carry the same entry fee. There are differences between levels of examination, GCSE, AS, A Level, but not within each suite. Yet the actual cost of running examinations varies enormously. The more the components, the more the marking, setting and revising fees. Some examinations involve the provision of taped material, which in the case of Music will incur copyright costs. Some require visiting examiners, or involve complex moderation procedures. And some attract such small candidatures that they have no hope of even covering their fixed costs. Serious commercial advice would urge Boards either to drop Russian, Greek and other minority subjects or to price them realistically.

Boards have regarded it as a principle that fees should not vary from syllabus to syllabus because they recognize that they provide a service and have a role to play in the education which young people receive. Discriminatory fees would mean that a number of subjects would cease to be taught in our schools. Could it be right for candidates to be told that they must choose their courses of study not from their aptitudes and interests but on the basis of what the subjects cost to examine? No Board has yet dared to take that step, although in some cases they are inching imperceptibly towards it by imposing surcharges, for instance when a visiting examiner is required. They announce their fee openly and bury such charges in the small print, often not noticed until the school bursar has to pay the final bill. Similarly the development of modular syllabuses, with the fees set per module, will push up the price actually paid, while the subject fee announced will be that for the non-modular syllabus and will sound modest. In fact the £50 A Level is already here if you look for it.

In defence of the Boards it is worth noting that examination entry fees are remarkably modest, especially considering their importance in the life and career of the candidates. GCSE costs between £15 and £17 per subject, depending on the Board of entry and whether discount for entry is available if made by electronic data interchange (EDI), while A Level varies from about £25 to £30. One wonders what candidates and their parents spend on theatre or restaurant visits, drinks or cigarettes, tapes or compact disks. You can stand in the rain and watch a couple of Third Division football matches or take a career-furthering GCSE. In terms of both cost to the Boards and value to the candidates, examinations are broadly underpriced.

It is worth asking briefly what backing and security a Board has if it falls into financial difficulties. Most of them are university foundations, going back to the second half of the nineteenth century. They were set up by their parent universities as a means of ensuring the standard of those students seeking places at the universities concerned. They were not originally tied in to any national system of education. Each school registered with a particular Board and entered candidates for the examinations which that Board offered. It is a relatively recent phenomenon for a school to spread its custom over several Boards, but now almost all do it.

Because their business was assured, with an established list of schools of whose candidates they could be certain, Boards had a stable financial environment. They could budget confidently and competition had no place. It was GCSE which broke the mould. When the Boards were combined into Groups, every school had to choose a new syllabus in every subject so that inertia could no longer reign, and old loyalties fell away. A school which might have stuck to the Oxford and Cambridge Board, for instance, felt less bound to the Midland Examining Group of which the Board had become a part.

Meanwhile the Boards' bonds with their parent universities had become little more than theoretical. There is no doubt that if the Boards did not exist, the universities would not now lift a finger to set them up. As it is, they would not wish to be seen to close them down but would probably do so if they were to become a financial burden. In Oxford when the Playhouse needed something like a quarter of a million pounds spending on it, the University closed it down. It took an independent trust to raise the necessary funds and open the Playhouse again. There is no reason to think that a university would be more tolerant towards an Examining Board, and even less to think that any independent trust would come into being to rescue a struggling Board.

THE BOARDS AND GOVERNMENT

This raises interesting thoughts on the relationship between the Examining Boards and the authorities which run British education, from the Secretary of State downwards. Educational policies are formed in which the Examining Boards are seen as an integral part. Their co-operation is taken for granted. Machinery is in place to approve the syllabuses which they offer and to monitor their operations. Nor could they take an independent line, even if they so wished, at least with pupils up to the age of 16, the age of compulsory education, in maintained schools. Such schools would simply not be allowed legally to enter their pupils for non-approved examinations. Of course Boards could offer any examinations they liked to independent schools, but such schools would be most unlikely to take so controversial a step. They have no wish to break from the mainstream of British education, nor to send their pupils out into the world with qualifications which might not be generally recognized. Thus the Examining Boards and the Department of Education have settled into a relationship which ignores the commercial facts.

If we ignore the independent sector, the whole of education (the supporting services as well as the schools) is state funded – and if the independent sector came to an end its pupils would be absorbed into the state system and so would be funded by the state. Only the Examining Boards are not so funded; yet they are treated as if they were. When new requirements are imposed upon them, such as syllabus development work to satisfy new criteria or to incorporate new subject cores, and when work done in good faith has to be scrapped and done again because of some change in the rules, probably announced without proper consultation and for political reasons, the cost has to be met by the Boards from fee income. And this has been a frequent occurrence. The restriction of coursework assessment to 20% of the whole, while perhaps well justified in many syllabuses, was announced by the then Prime Minister at a dinner not specifically concerned with education, and when syllabuses to which it had to apply had already been drafted. The requirement to allocate 5% of the marks for GCSE to spelling, punctuation and grammar, whatever its merits, was introduced in 1992 after the examination papers and mark-schemes to which it applied had been printed. In 1993 new A-Level syllabuses had to be written, in which there was a widespread desire for modular schemes to be introduced; however, the rules to govern such schemes were unknown because SEAC, as it then was (the present QCA), was unable to agree upon them.

In most spheres of public administration such muddle is a drain on central funds; in this case it was a blow to the Boards' funds and was bound eventually to have an impact on the entry fees paid by the candidates or the quality of service offered by the Boards, and arguably in some cases affected the very future of Boards themselves – as subsequent mergers have indicated.

This is not a plea for Examining Boards to be centrally funded. If they were, there is no doubt that they would become a cog in the official wheel. The independent advice (based upon profound expertise), which has had good effect in the shaping of policy, would wither away. But it is a plea for their true position to be recognized and possibly for a compromise to be reached whereby externally imposed demands are centrally funded while the Boards finance their own business operation – the running of examinations – from their own funds. Some such formalizing of the relationship between Government and the Boards seems desirable. If it does not come about, the day might arrive when a Board or Boards cut what they offer (no more syllabuses for minority interests), close down entirely, or even fail to deliver the results. At present there are, there can be, no guarantees. We know of travel agents closing down and leaving holiday-makers who have booked with them stranded; we never contemplate GCSE or A-Level candidates in the same position. But, however unlikely, it is not impossible as things are at present organized. An Examining Board is a commercial venture in the fullest sense of that term – and with all that it implies.

Chapter 2

How Does an Examining Board Work?

I have often heard disgruntled teachers say, 'Why on earth did the Board ... ?', whether complaining about what they saw as an unsatisfactory syllabus, a badly set question paper, or an administrative decision which they did not like. One of my favourite letters of complaint included the sentence, 'From the port-sodden fastnesses of which Oxford college did this question paper emanate?'

In fact the great majority of decisions, certainly the academic ones, stem from practising teachers. The setter of the 'port-sodden' question paper was Head of Department of a school very similar to that of the writer of the letter. They may well have met at conferences and found that their views broadly coincided, without identifying each other in connection with this particular crossing of swords. Boards have normally preferred to protect the anonymity of their examiners, although recently senior examiners have begun more and more to front training meetings, so that their identity is becoming known.

SENIOR MANAGEMENT

Examining Boards are run, theoretically at least, by a Board of Management (the specific title of which will vary from Board to Board). Since almost all Boards were university foundations this meant that in the early days they were managed by representatives of their universities, perhaps augmented by school representatives, probably headmasters. But these managing bodies did not meet frequently (perhaps only twice a year) and their members were in the best sense of the term amateurs. They did not have a day-to-day contact with the affairs of the Board and depended upon the information provided to them and the agenda prepared for their meetings by the Chief Executive (until recently with the title of Secretary). In my early involvement I formed the clear impression that the Chief Executive *was* the Board. He (or occasionally she) prepared agendas and could usually ensure that he got the decisions he wanted. Frequently decisions had to be taken in the long gaps between meetings, and there was never any serious doubt that they would be ratified retrospectively.

The Chief Executives themselves were normally recruited from the teaching profession, probably at headteacher level or at least of considerable seniority. There was no doubt of their capacity to run their Boards from an academic point of view and to relate appropriately to the schools which entered candidates and to the examiners whom they employed. As long as their Boards did not fall into financial difficulties they would be left, with only minor supervision, to get on with the job.

The best members of the Boards of Management would themselves serve as examiners. This gave them an invaluable insight into the work of the Board which they were required to help manage. At the same time it created a curious relationship with the Chief Executive: on the one hand they would have been involved in his appointment and could presumably dismiss him; on the other, he appointed them as examiners and could dismiss them from that post.

Since the mid-'80s this structure has become more professional. Boards have merged and so become larger. The Chief Executive is now more likely to be recruited from business or industry, from the world of professional management. The computer has taken over, and Boards depend upon a large staff of information technology experts. The complexities of employment law have given rise to personnel departments. Competition has led to the setting up of marketing departments. The old pattern of a Secretary supported by a Finance Officer (quite possibly without professional qualifications) and a small team of clerical staff has gone for good. An Examining Board today is precisely like any other large commercial organization.

At the same time the Board of Management will almost certainly no longer include any examiners, and university representation is not large, as universities have reduced their involvement with the Boards, even when nominally it still exists. Professional expertise is required, so that a Chief Education Officer would be a prized member of such a Board, and teaching unions are likely to have a significant input. Boards are likely to meet quite frequently, and to be dealing with national issues, the evolution of public examinations in the widest sense and the relationship of the Board to the regulatory body. Its financial stability is now a matter of permanent concern, whereas it could once have been taken for granted. Day-to-day issues of any particular examination, matters of primary interest to schools and candidates, are dealt with further down the line.

ACADEMIC MANAGEMENT

Below the senior committee there will be an Examinations Committee. This body will be responsible to the Board of Management for academic matters. It will recommend which subjects, and how many syllabuses in each, should be offered, and it will decide and monitor the procedures for the conduct of the Board's examinations. It is of course increasingly subject to nationally imposed criteria for syllabuses and nationally agreed procedures through a Code of Practice. Nevertheless, the Examinations Committee has extensive decision-making responsibility within its Board. It remains composed almost entirely of practising teachers, some nominated by Teachers' Associations, some appointed by geographically based consultative committees. A few may be recently retired teachers and there may be a small number of representatives of higher education to ensure a logical relationship from one stage of education to the next. However, the key is that this body above all represents the teachers. Its decisions should turn out to be welcome to the teaching profession, and when anyone says, 'Why on earth did the Board . . . ?' she should rather be saying, 'Why on earth did my professional colleagues . . . ?'. If she saw her own question in that light she might end by wondering whether it is she herself who is wrong.

Below the Examinations Committee is a range of Subject Committees. There will be a separate committee for each major subject or subject area: thus English will cover both Language and Literature; Electronics will be subsumed into Physics (which may in any case be subsumed itself into a Science committee), and Geology probably into Geography; a single committee will embrace all the Modern Languages. All members of these committees are likely to be practising teachers. Any who are not will certainly have a very close and recent involvement with the profession. They are recruited as widely as possible so that all aspects of the committee's responsibility are covered, and also the whole range of the candidature. The ideal is that for each syllabus or syllabus option there will be someone who teaches it; for each type of school – maintained or independent, boarding or day, mixed or single sex, full age range or sixth-form college – there will be someone who teaches there. So far as possible, members will be typical teachers, not selected because they have come to notice for unusual views or bombarded the Board with letters. Again, if a teacher is unhappy with a syllabus he should realize that he is complaining about decisions of as normal a cross-section of his colleagues as the Board has been able to find.

It is these Subject Committees which decide the syllabuses in their every detail (subject only to conformity with national criteria). They receive and consider letters of criticism or suggestion and respond as appropriate. They take active steps when important decisions have to be taken to consult more widely, perhaps by consultation meetings open to all teachers of their subject or by questionnaires circulated to all schools. Their final decisions should not reflect the views of any forceful individual but be a true consensus of the views of teachers.

THE EXAMINERS

The real work is of course that done by the examiners, both the Chief (who has overall responsibility for a syllabus) and Principal Examiners (who each have overall responsibility for a single component) in setting the question papers, and the Assistant Examiners in marking the scripts. These all are, or very recently have been, active teachers of the subject, and very probably the precise syllabus, which they are examining. The quality controls to which they are themselves subject will be covered in the next chapter. But of course through teaching the subject and preparing their own pupils for the same or parallel public examinations, they are fully aware of what can fairly be expected, how questions can best be worded to enable candidates to show their paces, and what perhaps moderate or even weak candidates are trying to say and so what marks they deserve. It is this day-to-day teaching work with real candidates which qualifies them to be sensitive examiners with the rightly tuned level of judgement.

In the light of the above one must pause to ask how examiners who are setting question papers can honestly prepare candidates to take them. It would be all too easy to include in mock examinations or school tests questions which they knew will appear in the live papers. It is of course a matter of integrity. My own perception is that being taught by the setter of a question paper is more likely to hinder than to help a candidate. A teacher who does not know what questions will appear may by chance hit upon one in preparing the candidates: question-spotting is something which most teachers try to do. But the setter of the paper will in fact make a point of not spotting questions which he knows are on the paper. Thus his pupils can never have the benefit of a lucky guess. I have twice met allegations of a teacher leaking information to his own pupils. Neither case was substantiated, nor did the work of the candidates concerned suggest that they had had any prior knowledge of the questions. Any examiner who was found to have betrayed this trust would not only be dismissed as an examiner by the Board, but would also almost certainly be dismissed from the teaching profession for gross professional misconduct: his career would be at an end. Few, and one hopes none, will take that risk, while for the Board the advantages of having the papers set by active teachers far outweigh whatever small risk there is.

As a footnote, and to set against the suggestion that being taught by a setter might be a disadvantage, I am sure that candidates gain if they are taught by someone directly involved in examining. The teacher is ideally equipped to advise on examination technique, on the sort of things which gain marks and the ways in which marks are lost. None of these things are secret from the profession as a whole; the Boards publish their mark-schemes and accompany them with detailed reports on each examination, so that lessons can be learned. But the teacher who has put them into practice as an examiner will appreciate and communicate them better than one who has merely read about them. If I were a headteacher I should want at least one teacher in each department to be an examiner with the Board for which the school enters candidates.

The key figures, however, in this whole structure are the Chief and Principal Examiners (or Awarders, as some Boards called them until the Code of Practice standardized their titles). This is not only because they set the question papers, write the mark-schemes and standardize the Assistant Examiners; it is because they are the only people who are able to gain an overall perspective of how an examination has worked. Their influence when grading decisions are taken (a procedure described in Chapter 4) is by far the most important; the subject report which they write and which is issued to all centres which entered candidates is the Board's most direct way of communicating with centres; they almost certainly will front INSET meetings with teachers; their recommendations to the Subject Committee will carry very great weight. In consequence, modifications to syllabuses, other than those stemming from central revision of national criteria, almost always stem from the Chief and Principal Examiners (and Moderators in the case of coursework).

Since the mid-'90s the work of Chief Examiners has been under the oversight of a Chair of Examiners. The Code of Practice introduced this role primarily in a bid to achieve a uniform standard in cases where a Board had more than one syllabus in the same subject. Proliferation of syllabuses arose partly from project bodies: thus there are the Nuffield and Salters suites of syllabuses in the Sciences and the MEI and SMP syllabuses in Mathematics. It also increased when modular alternatives to the traditional linear syllabuses became popular. The function of the Chair of Examiners is primarily to take the Chair at the meetings at which question papers are finalized and at which grade boundaries are set. The burden of work would make it impossible for an examiner to set and mark in more than one syllabus, but the Chair, who personally does neither of these tasks, has time to bring an eye to bear across the full range of the subject. He or she must be satisfied, for instance, that the question papers set in MEI Mathematics, SMP Mathematics and traditional Mathematics are of equal demand, and that the grade boundaries eventually agreed represent the same standard of attainment in each syllabus.

The role requires considerable subject expertise and clear awareness of standards established over time. It is best carried out by a former senior examiner with long experience in the details of the whole process. Even so, no one person will have an equal grasp of every option in the subject; no one person will have taught or examined all the options. The role requires a broad understanding, almost an instinct, and a very good relationship with the different Chief Examiners being supervised. If the Chair is satisfied that standards in the syllabuses within his remit are out of line, it may be necessary to insist that one or other of the teams makes an adjustment, but it is much better to be able to convince the errant team and bring them into line by persuasion and a clear demonstration of the discrepancy. Only in that way will a proper baseline be established for the future.

SUBJECT ADMINISTRATION

At subject level all the administration is linked together by the Subject Officer. This person is usually, but not always, a specialist in the subject for which he or she is responsible. Inevitably specialist knowledge cannot be complete. Thus the officer responsible for Modern Languages might be fluent in French and German but have no knowledge of Spanish or Russian; an officer might deal with three or four humanities subjects while being a specialist in only one; an expert in Physics might also be responsible for Chemistry and Biology. The primary role of the job is administrative, i.e. to:

- ensure that the schedule for the production of question papers is met;
- prepare agenda papers, write minutes and implement decisions of meetings of the Subject Committee and its sub-committees;
- organize and service the standardization of marking, and the grading and grade review procedures;
- deal with all routine correspondence and telephone communication from Centres, insofar as it relates directly to the subject.

Normally Subject Officers are former teachers, but there have been more cases recently where this is not so, as the demands of administration become more important and more complex. It is certainly a role which does not demand subject knowledge, but I have no doubt that a subject specialist will do the job much better, even if only at the level of being able to spot typographical errors in a question paper which have been overlooked by those who should have noticed them. Centres certainly expect the Subject Officer to be a specialist, and if they telephone with a query about a technical point in the subject they expect to speak to someone who will know the answer, rather than to be told that the question will have to be referred to the Chief Examiner and that they might get an answer in a week or so. I recall talking to a teacher at a meeting of History teachers who told me that his school had changed the Board with which it entered candidates in History simply because he had discovered that the Subject Officer in their original Board was not a historian. If the officer is both a former teacher and a subject specialist he, and nowadays increasingly she, will be able to establish the best rapport with the centres, provide the service they want, and win their confidence to the benefit of all concerned.

EXTERNAL INPUT

As the previous chapter showed, Boards are very anxious to provide what the customers want. Thus, although the structure described is formal and detailed, with a system of checks and balances, informal input from centres is never ignored and is a genuine factor in how a Board works. If a Board received a significant number of letters criticizing details of a syllabus or details of administration, or a number of suggestions for change, they would certainly be given the fullest consideration.

Similarly the Boards are always eager to relate to subject-specific professional bodies. In the past such bodies, of which the Nuffield Foundation is a good example, have been a fruitful source of innovation in approaches to teaching, and have generated new syllabuses which have required tailor-made assessment. In the early days one Board would examine such a syllabus but, as an exception to the normal practice, would allow access to the examination to candidates entering via other Boards. Recently, as national criteria have become central, and as the Boards have merged into larger units, the syllabuses have become the property of the Boards, with input from the relevant project body, rather than the property of the project body with the work of examination undertaken by a Board. The acceptance by the conducting Board of entries via another Board no longer happens. Thus the project bodies have become increasingly sidelined, although their input upon teaching, particularly in Mathematics and the Sciences, but also in a range of other subjects, including History, Classics and Economics, has been enormous.

The message of this chapter is that an Examining Board is an increasingly complex administrative machine, that its procedures have become increasingly formal and subject to ever-closer outside supervision, but that its roots lie in the teaching profession. The decisions which really matter and which govern its central purpose – producing an appropriate syllabus and setting an examination of the proper standard upon it – are still firmly in the hands of practising teachers.

Chapter 3

The Instruments of Measurement: Question Papers and Marks

WHAT DOES AN EXAMINATION RESULT REPRESENT?

To appreciate much of what follows it will be useful to establish what an examination result actually represents. Results are assumed automatically by the public at large to have an absolute validity. The grade awarded to the candidate is accepted as a definitive evaluation of the candidate's ability, attainment, potential, or indeed whatever qualities the user values. This is of course spurious. An examination result records the judgement of one particular examiner upon the work produced by the candidate on a particular day in a particular set of circumstances. A little more precisely – since virtually all examinations involve more than one examination paper or component – the result records the aggregation of several such individual judgements upon particular pieces of work each produced on a particular day in particular circumstances.

One can of course put a little more value on the result than that if the examination has been properly run. With the different examiners efficiently standardized to a well-written mark-scheme, the result ought to reflect the judgement which any member of the examining team, not just the one who marked the script, would have made upon that particular work. Moreover, since the grading decisions, which follow on from the marking, will have been taken by the judgement of a team of the most senior examining personnel, following a procedure to be described in the next chapter, the grade awarded to the candidate records the judgement made by that team upon that work. They will probably not have seen the work itself, but if not they will have seen work carrying the same mark value, and will have made a judgement upon the grade value of work carrying that mark. Even so, it remains a judgement made on particular work produced on a particular day or days in a particular set of circumstances.

There is no evidence that, because a particular result has been produced, the candidate could replicate that result. A second attempt, on a different day in a different set of circumstances, might be quite different, whether for better or worse. In other fields of human endeavour we should not expect a single performance to be definitive. An athlete who runs a race in a particular time, jumps a particular height, or throws a missile a particular distance would be most unlikely to repeat the performance precisely on every occasion. Indeed the athlete who sets a world record very rarely, and probably never, repeats the performance. If one performance were definitive, sporting events would be meaningless; one would know the results in advance. All that one result tells us is that the athlete (candidate) is capable of performing at that standard; he or she might never again reach those heights (or sink to those depths).

It follows that users of examination results should use them with caution. A university admissions tutor or potential employer ought to look at any other information available, and above all at a full report from the school which, if honest, ought to set the result in context and indicate whether it marked a high or low point, or quite possibly the norm, of the candidate's performance.

THE RELATIVE DIFFICULTY OF QUESTIONS

Let us then consider the instruments of measurement used to assess this performance. First we need to note the lack of precision in these instruments of measurement. To maintain the analogy with athletics, the event is the examination paper while the timing or measuring mechanism is the marks awarded. However, the length of a metre, the duration of a second, have fixed validity; they are universally known. But no two examination papers are identical and the value of a mark is what the examiner says it is.

It is the declared aim of the Examining Boards to maintain the same standard of examination papers from year to year. The problem lies in demonstrating that this is so. The relative difficulty of any two questions is probably a matter of opinion. At a very simple level, is 7 × 8 easier or harder than 6 × 9? It would be possible to put the two questions to a large number of children and to decide between them on the basis of which was answered correctly the more often; but without such research I doubt if anyone can pronounce with total confidence on the relative difficulty of two questions as straightforward as those.

At a higher level, consider two possible questions suitable for A-Level English Literature: *Discuss Shakespeare's characterization of Hamlet* and *Discuss Shakespeare's characterization of Macbeth*. On the surface these might appear to be of equal difficulty. However, one play is much longer than the other, one character has much more to say than the other, the events of the play, the number and behaviour of the other characters with whom the protagonist has to react are quite different. And even when one has recognized that one play is more substantial than the other, I am not sure whether the question upon it is thereby easier or harder. Having more to say might make it easier for the candidate to write something, but harder to cover all the ground. These inevitable inequalities in questions have to be dealt with via the mark-scheme.

I am sure that in every subject, questions can be set which are superficially identical; but the moment one considers what the candidates might write in reply, inequalities emerge. There is even scope for disagreement about the type of questions which are easy or difficult. It seems to be widely believed that factual questions are easy and that evaluative questions are hard. In fact the hardest question on earth is the factual question to which one does not know the answer; the easiest is that to which one does. Thus the same question will be impossible for some candidates and a give-away to others. As for evaluative questions, it might be difficult to score full marks, but even the weakest candidate can probably write something worthy of at least a modest mark. Consider the following: *Who was Henry VIII's second wife?* This is easy if you know it and impossible if you have forgotten the name. But as for *Did Henry VIII treat Ann Boleyn fairly?*, every candidate who has studied the period is likely to write something relevant and plausible, some more fully and others less so.

SETTING A QUESTION PAPER

The procedure for setting a question paper is carefully set out. First, a draft is produced by the Principal Examiner. This draft is sent to Revisers, normally two, whose job it is to find fault if at all possible. If a question is too hard or too easy (in their opinion – see above), if it is ambiguous or badly worded, if it overlaps with another question on the paper or is too similar to one set in the previous session, it is their role to say so. In the light of their comments the Principal Examiner amends the draft and a meeting is held at which the paper will be finalized. The Chair of Examiners is responsible for this meeting, and the Chief Examiner, all the Principal Examiners for the syllabus, and the Revisers will be present. The question papers are discussed in detail, often over many hours, until a version is produced which all present agree is of the correct standard.

Even after this there remains one more hurdle. The final version is sent to an Assessor, someone who has not yet had a hand in the process and has therefore not seen the paper in draft form. The Assessor's role is to act as a candidate and work the paper. He will then compare his own answers with those on the mark-scheme. If an answer is different from that which the mark-scheme expected, this may well indicate an ambiguity in the question paper which the team, for all its lengthy consideration, had not noticed. The Assessor is also invaluable in detecting typographical errors. I recall a case of a Geography paper, in the days before Assessors were used, in which the question originally set had been changed at the meeting but the map reference printed on the question paper had not been amended to correspond. An Assessor would have realized that the question as printed was impossible and it would have been sorted out before being placed in front of the candidates.

The question paper which finally emerges is one which the most experienced team that the Board can muster agrees is fair and of the correct standard, the same standard as in previous years. But even so it remains only a matter of opinion, however good the grounds may be for trusting that opinion.

PRE-TESTING QUESTIONS

One may reasonably ask what scope there is for researching question difficulty and using pre-tested questions to construct examination papers. For multiple-choice papers this is standard practice. However, these questions are easy to process. Each question is accompanied by four or five suggested answers, only one of which is correct. The candidate is required to tick the correct answer. The ticks can be machine-read and statistics produced to measure their ease or difficulty. Pre-tested questions are banked, and when a paper is to be set, questions of the required difficulty can be chosen. But if one wishes to use questions requiring a more complex answer, and in particular if the answer is to be in the form of an essay, pre-testing is not a practicable option. It would require detailed marking by examiners, who are increasingly difficult to recruit for live examinations, let alone for research purposes (and it would of course involve most of the costs of a live examination without producing any income). Their marking would have to be standardized and checked, and some form of grading decisions taken to interpret what the marks mean; this is quite different from answers which are right or wrong. Nor would the Boards so easily find candidates willing to act as guinea pigs for such papers. A pre-test of a multiple-choice paper is usually quite short, so that a school can fit it into a normal teaching lesson without disruption to its timetable. Schools are often quite willing to allow their pupils to be used in this way shortly before a live examination as useful practice and a helpful element in revision, since many short questions can give wide coverage of the syllabus. They would be less happy, I suspect, to organize anything longer in its time demand but probably narrower in its coverage. Moreover, in some subjects syllabus content changes from year to year. This is most obvious in subjects involving literature. Thus in English the prescribed works change frequently, and if one wanted to pre-test questions on a book to be set a few years ahead there would be no students reading it on whom questions could be tested.

On balance pre-testing has been rejected as a method of evaluating questions, except for multiple-choice papers, which in most subjects would not be an appropriate way of assessing the skills which the candidate is required to show.

WEIGHTED MARKS

The second instrument of measurement is the mark-scheme. It is usually a matter of astonishment to those not intimately involved in examining to learn that a mark is not always a mark! Examiners mark questions and papers out of a mark total which is convenient, but the raw total on that paper may not be the correct total to give that component the weighting which it is required to have relative to the other components. I was myself once involved with a syllabus consisting of four components whose final weightings had to be 25%, 25%, 30% and 20% respectively. However, the raw mark totals out of which the papers were marked were 66, 66, 99 and 100. This was a matter of convenience to fit the nature of the work being marked and to enable the examiners to work with mark totals which could easily be matched to the assessment objectives without having to deal in fractions. To achieve the required weightings we had to convert each 66 to 50, the 99 to 60 and the 100 to 40. Thus on the first two components one raw mark was actually worth 0.76, on the third it was worth 0.61, and on the fourth 0.4.

This gave rise to what at first sight might have been thought to be unjust outcomes. To take an example (selecting numbers for which the calculations are fairly easy): imagine two candidates whose raw scores on the four components described above were respectively $25 + 25 + 25 + 75 = 150$ and $33 + 33 + 33 + 50 = 149$. The final performance seems to be virtually identical, with the first candidate marginally better. But when these raw marks are converted to their final values they become respectively $19 + 19 + 15.25 + 30 = 83.25$ (83 to the nearest whole mark) and $25 + 25 + 20 + 20 = 90$. The second candidate is now markedly better than the first, and if a grade boundary falls anywhere between 84 and 90 this candidate will obtain a higher grade.

In fact this is not unjust, since the syllabus will have been planned with the clear perception that marks are easier to obtain on some components than on others (not necessarily because the questions are easier, but perhaps because the marking is more generous). It follows that a mark gained on an easy component will not be worth as much as a mark gained on a harder component. As an integral feature of the syllabus this will be known to the candidates and their teachers before the examination, and an apparently anomalous outcome should not surprise them. In the syllabus described above, the component carrying 100 raw marks was coursework. It was thought to enable markers to apply the marking criteria more easily if they had plenty of marks to allocate under each criterion, so that in the interest of accurate and reliable marking and good discrimination a raw total of 100 was allocated. Whether this was right or necessary may be worthy of debate; but once the decision has been taken the mathematical oddities are inevitable – and not unjust.

THE UNIFORM MARK SCALE

There is, however, one form of mathematical adjustment of marks which, in my opinion, is manifestly unjust and which, I have no doubt, has led to incorrect grades being awarded. This is the conversion of raw marks awarded in modular syllabuses to the Uniform Mark Scale (UMS).

The key problem in awarding final grades in a modular syllabus is that a candidate may have taken modules spread over several sessions, and grade boundaries can change from session to session as the papers set are perceived to be marginally harder or marginally easier. If a candidate took a module in the first year, scored 70%, and the grade A boundary happened to be set at 70%, how would that performance be treated if in the year in which the candidate wished to be graded, a paper of a different standard had been set and the boundary had accordingly been adjusted to 75%? The candidate is clearly worthy of grade A, but if the original mark were left at 70, grade A would not be awarded. For this reason raw marks in any modular scheme are converted to the UMS in order to achieve consistency.

The total UMS marks available in an A-Level modular scheme are 600 (for AS the total is 300). This is because the commonest modular pattern is to have six equally weighted modules to each of which 100 UMS marks can be allocated. If a syllabus consisted of four equal modules each would carry 150 UMS marks; a three-module scheme weighted respectively at 50%, 30% and 20% would see the modules carrying 300, 180 and 120 UMS marks. Many combinations are possible and have been in use in recent years, although the new syllabuses due to be examined (as at present expected) in 2001 for AS and 2002 for A Level will all consist of six modules.

In this scheme, wherever the boundaries are set in terms of raw marks, boundaries on the UMS scale are set at 80% for grade A, 70% for B, 60% for C, and so on, dropping 10% per grade. On the basic pattern of six equal modules each worth 100 UMS marks, and for convenience assuming that the raw mark maximum was also 100, if the agreed raw boundaries were 75 for grade A, 66 for B, 58 for C, 51 for D, 44 for E and 37 for N, these would convert to 80, 70, 60, 50, 40 and 30 respectively. It is at once apparent that the raw marks have been stretched. The candidate who scored 75 will be given 80 UMS marks, while the candidate who scored 37 will see that mark reduced to 30 by the UMS conversion (to him who hath shall be given; from him who hath not shall be taken away!).

Secondly, raw marks have a different UMS value depending upon where they fall on the scale. Raw marks falling between 100 and 75 will be mapped on a range from 100 to 80, i.e. each raw mark will be worth 0.8 of a UMS mark. A raw mark of 66 converts to 70, with a range of 75–66 becoming 80–70 and each raw mark therefore worth 0.9 of a UMS mark. In the remaining bands a raw mark is worth 0.8, 0.7, 0.7, 0.7 and 0.8 (the band below N) respectively. These differences may seem trivial, but there are always candidates a mark below any grade boundary, and the mark lost may have been caused by the variation of 0.1 per mark over 10 marks. That a raw mark may be worth 0.9, 0.8 or 0.7 of a UMS mark, depending upon where the candidate's score falls in relation to the grade boundary, cannot be right.

Modular schemes were pioneered in the main by Mathematics and the Sciences. In these subjects high marks, even full marks, are very possible. The A boundary could well be set at 80%, or at least not far off. If the real boundaries match the UMS boundaries the conversion will be exact, and if they are close adjustments will be minor, and may be consistent across the mark range. But in arts subjects examiners are much less likely to award full, or very high marks. A History or English essay marked out of 25 will see hardly any candidate scoring above 20 or below 8. The consequence is that the A boundary could well be set in the low 60s with the N boundary in the 30s, and therefore very narrow grade bands. Again to choose numbers convenient for calculation, consider the figures shown in Table 3.1.

Table 3.1

Grade	Raw mark boundary	UMS boundary	UMS value of 1 raw mark
A	60	80	0.5
B	55	70	2
C	50	60	2
D	45	50	2
E	40	40	2
N	35	30	2
	0	0	0.86

Again let us compare two candidates. The one scores 60 raw marks on each of the six modules, a raw total of 360, each converting to 80 UMS marks, a total of 480 and a grade A. The second scores 61 raw marks on each of four modules and 59 on the other two, a raw total of 362. Each 61 converts to 80.5 UMS marks, while each 59 converts to 78. This gives a total of 478 UMS marks and a final grade of B. Yet it appears logical that the second candidate was better than the first, if not by much. While it may be acceptable for marks scored on different components to have a different final value, if the writers of the syllabus so design it and explicitly publish it, it cannot be right for a mark on one and the same component to be of a different value according to where it falls within the range. No syllabus writer, no examiner, ever intended that or published it as a feature of any syllabus ever written.

When a module carries a greater weighting than 100 UMS marks the anomalies become even greater. A module worth 50% of the final weighting would have its raw marks converted to a UMS maximum of 300 (with A at 240, B at 210 and so on, descending by 30 marks per grade). If the module were itself only marked out of 100 and the raw boundaries were those postulated by the figures set out in the table above, we should have the results shown in Table 3.2.

Table 3.2

Grade	Raw mark boundary	UMS boundary	UMS value of 1 raw mark
A	60	240	1.5
B	55	210	6
C	50	180	6
D	45	150	6
E	40	120	6
N	35	90	6
	0	0	2.57

The possibility of a candidate with a lower raw total obtaining a higher grade than one with a higher raw total has now increased significantly, since for every raw mark below the A boundary on one module the candidate must score 4 raw marks above the A boundary elsewhere to compensate.

The anomaly described above existed in its full virulence at AS and A Level up to and including 1997. It was a scheme agreed by all the Examining Boards and the School Curriculum and Assessment Authority (SCAA) jointly. By the time of the 1998 examination the Boards and the Qualifications and Curriculum Authority (QCA), which had replaced SCAA as the regulatory body, had become aware of the problem and had made an adjustment designed to overcome it. They decreed that in 1998 (and thereafter unless new councils prevail) a ceiling would be set on the raw mark maximum as far above the A boundary mark as the B boundary mark is below it. Thus, if A were set at 65 and B at 57, a gap of 8 raw marks, the raw maximum for UMS calculation purposes would be set at 73. This certainly has the effect that a mark above the A boundary will carry the same UMS value as a mark below it. The disadvantage is that a candidate who scores a raw mark above this artificially imposed maximum gains no benefit from so doing. On the figures above, 73 converts to 100 UMS marks (I am assuming six equal modules for purposes of this example) as does any mark above 73, giving 27 raw marks (74–100) which are of no value.

It is argued that a candidate so able as to score above the new theoretical maximum will in any case be good enough to gain grade A at syllabus level: but this is not necessarily so. While a candidate in this position already has 20 UMS marks in hand above the A boundary there remain five modules in which those 20 marks can easily be lost. Depending on the placing of the boundaries, and so the conversion value of the marks, a couple of marks per module short of the A boundary on the other modules could see the candidate losing a grade which would have been gained if the surplus marks on the one strong module had been allowed to count. I know from my own experience that in 1998 there were candidates who suffered in this way.

ALLOCATING MARKS TO OBJECTIVES AND QUESTIONS

Having shown that a raw mark may have its value affected by the weighting of the component, and that its value may be reduced or inflated in modular schemes by the UMS conversion, we come to the more basic point that the examiners have to decide initially what is worth a mark. When a syllabus is written the assessment objectives are identified and weighted. A question may assess three objectives: let us say, factual knowledge, understanding, coherent presentation of the material. Someone will have decided to weight these, 40, 40, 20, or 45, 30, 25, or 50, 35, 15, or whatever combination seems appropriate to the material and to the total mark available. But this relative weighting of skills is and has to be a matter of opinion. The opinion may be that of the best subject experts available, but it remains opinion, and it affects the results of the candidates. A candidate who has outstanding factual recall but little else will benefit if that objective is more highly weighted, while the candidate who writes well and has a good grasp of the subject, but who makes several factual errors or omissions, will benefit if his strengths are favoured by the weighting.

Similarly, in setting specific questions, the examiners' decisions influence the outcome. A common pattern, especially in GCSE, is to provide a stimulus, which may take the form of a picture, plan, diagram or short passage of written material, and to set a series of low-tariff questions based upon it. Usually the value of the questions rises from a single-mark opener to a summary question worth perhaps five or six marks. The examiner will decide which questions are easy, and so lightly rewarded, and which are of greater value. I have taken part in many meetings where examiners have discussed the values to be put on such questions, and I have realized that the decisions will affect the grades gained by individual candidates. A higher mark may be put on a question to which the candidate knows the answer and a lower mark on one to which he does not, while to another candidate the reverse is true. Had the examiners' decision gone the other way the relative outcome for the two candidates, at that minor level, would have changed.

THE MARK-SCHEME

The standardization of the examining team also has its effect. At a very early stage in the marking process, when the examiners have marked a few scripts (sufficient to give them a sense of how the candidates have responded), the full examining team meets. They work through the mark-scheme, question by question, to satisfy themselves that in the light of the scripts which they have seen the scheme is working fairly. At this point alternative answers which candidates have actually written, but which had not been anticipated by the original mark-scheme, are discussed, and their acceptability – and value if accepted – are decided. It is usually a matter of opinion whether such answers are of any value. But to the candidate it may be of critical importance whether such an answer is allowed to have full marks, half marks, or not to be credited at all.

It is at this stage too that the exact awarding of marks is determined. In long essays in particular few candidates, if any, will write everything that there is to be written. So must there be, say, ten good points for full marks, or will eight be sufficient? The examiners' decision, when they see what candidates are actually doing, will again be decisive to the final grade for some who are on the borderline.

From all the above it can be seen how crucial the mark-scheme is in establishing the standard of the examination. It can be constructed to allow for the variable difficulty of questions. If when the scripts are marked a question is seen not to have worked well, to have been too difficult, or ambiguous, the mark-scheme can be adjusted to allow for that. It is a flexible instrument designed to ensure that the candidates are properly rewarded in mark terms for their efforts.

Chapter 4

Grading the Candidates

Having noted how variable are the instruments of measurement, we come to the final and decisive variable, the grade boundaries. It is still possible to rescue a bad paper and a bad mark-scheme if this job can be done well. If the paper has been disastrously dificult, for instance, and it has not even been possible to construct a mark-scheme which gives the candidates many marks, it is still possible to rescue the situation by setting very low boundaries, however embarrassing the implications may be for the Board (and one can imagine what the press might say). The only change which cannot be made by the grading process is to alter the order of merit of the candidates: that is one factor which the marking has had to get right unaided.

RECOMMENDING THE BOUNDARIES

The grading decisions are taken by a committee under the Chair of Examiners. The Subject Officer will be responsible for the provision of all the required materials. The Chief Examiner and Principal Examiners are key participants, and suitably qualified members of the Subject Committee may also be involved if the Board sees fit.

For each component the Principal Examiner is required to recommend a range of marks within which each judgemental boundary is likely in his opinion to fall. (For GCSE these judgemental boundaries are A, C and F, while for A Level they are A, B and E.) Prior to making this recommendation he should have studied the archive scripts, kept by the Board from the previous year, to attune his mind to the established standard, which it is the object of the exercise to replicate. However, I have to admit that once again we are into the realm of opinion, or rather of judgement, and not of fact. Reading the answers written on one question paper and seeing what grade value was put upon it only in the vaguest way enables one to make a judgement about answers written upon quite different questions. It seems to me like comparing an apple and a pear. One can weigh and measure them, just as one can add up the marks on an examination script, but if differences are small no measurement can tell you which is 'better'. Even so, it would be a dereliction of duty not to look at past evidence and to absorb from it whatever impressions one can.

STATISTICAL POINTERS

The Subject Officer and Chair of Examiners will consider the recommendations of the Principal Examiners and will note any other relevant evidence. One factor will be the forecast grades submitted by the centres. Do the centres believe that the candidates whom they are entering this year are better or worse than last? On the whole centres forecast well, although they will tend to be optimistic. If they feel that a candidate is borderline and they are not sure whether to forecast, say, B or C, they will almost certainly opt for the higher. It generally turns out in most subjects that final results are a little below centre forecasts, but not much. A second factor is the mean mark scored on the component. If the mean mark is higher than in the previous year it follows either that the candidates are better or that the paper is easier. If the centre forecasts suggest poorer candidates and yet the mean mark has gone up there will be reasonable grounds for concluding that the paper has been easier and so for expecting the grade boundaries to rise by a few marks in comparison with the previous year. In reverse, forecasts suggesting a stronger field coupled with a lower mean mark would imply that the paper has been hard and that the boundaries should be eased accordingly.

The Subject Officer and Chair of Examiners will also work out several possible outcomes. These will usually include what the final outcome would be if the previous year's boundaries were used, what it would be if the mid-point of the ranges recommended by the Principal Examiners were used, and probably the outcome arising from boundaries suggested by the consideration of forecast grades and mean marks.

The plausibility of these possible outcomes will be judged in comparison with the previous year's final outcome. It is not the Boards' intention, nor would it be right, to allow statistics to over-ride judgement. If statistics were all, one could simply set the grade boundaries at the figure which would generate the same percentage of grades A, B, C, etc. as in the previous year. Meetings and detailed consideration of scripts would be unnecessary. But equally judgement cannot ignore statistical pointers. If in the judgement of the examiners there were massive swings, for better or worse, of candidates gaining top grades, or of candidates failing, one would have to question that judgement. In large-entry subjects one would expect the results to be stable. Again to take a parallel with athletics, if one were to ask how many 16-year-olds can run 100 metres in twelve seconds one would not expect the answer to vary much from year to year. Why then should one expect the answer to vary much from year to year in, say, GCSE English or Mathematics?

THE EVIDENCE OF THE SCRIPTS

Having assessed these possible outcomes, the Subject Officer and Chair of Examiners will decide the range of scripts to be considered by the Grading Committee. This range would be expected to be that originally recommended by the Principal Examiners, but may have been adjusted at one end or the other to take account of the other pointers discussed above. It will need to be a reasonably wide range, since the expectation is that the scripts at the top of the range will be indisputably of the higher grade, and those at the bottom indisputably of the lower, to provide an anchor at each end of the range to be discussed. In most circumstances I should expect a range of no fewer than six marks, although for a component carrying a low total mark, for example 40, the grade bands themselves will be so narrow that the range of scripts to be considered spanning a grade boundary would probably be small. In practice components with a small mark total give poor discrimination and are hard to handle in grading, when perhaps as few as three or four marks might separate bottom A from top C.

The grading procedures require there to be a reasonable number of scripts available for perusal on every mark across the chosen range. Ideally one would have sufficient for each member of the Grading Committee to have a script to read, so that no one is sitting with nothing to do. In a large-entry subject with a normal distribution of marks this is not a problem. However, in a highly selective subject (A-Level Greek and Russian spring to mind) there may be very few scripts at the lowest boundary, and sometimes on a particular mark there may be none at all. In such circumstances, if a judgemental decision cannot be taken, because there is inadequate evidence on which to take it, statistical evidence will have to prevail.

If at all possible the scripts should also represent a performance of consistent standard across all the questions. At the top and bottom grades this is usually true of most scripts; even so a good candidate might have written, say, three very good answers and one weak one, or a poor candidate one good answer on an otherwise poor paper. One of the most difficult judgements to make is to determine how far one question out of line with the others should affect the overall grade. At a middle level (and for GCSE the C boundary is decided judgementally) the whole performance may be erratic, with no single answer of grade C standard. For instance, if one were looking at scripts carrying 50 marks and felt this to be the likely C grade boundary, a script carrying 13 + 13 + 12 + 12 for its four answers would truly reflect the standard, but a script carrying $19 + 19 + 6 + 6$ would probably represent work of grade A and grade E standard, but none at grade C. How then could it be used to identify grade C work?

EXERCISING JUDGEMENT

With all the required scripts before them the Grading Committee can begin its deliberations. Once again experts are to make judgements, and it would be hopelessly idealistic to expect that they will agree in every detail. I do not believe that it is possible to look at two scripts one mark apart and to identify that they deserve to be of a different grade. I have known examiners read two scripts carrying the same mark, agree that the scripts have been marked correctly, and yet have a feeling that one is better than the other. I have even known examiners read two scripts one mark apart and, while still agreeing that the two have been marked correctly, express a preference for the one with the lower mark.

So far as possible marking is precise. Marks can be given one by one, sentence by sentence, in some subjects even word by word or digit by digit. In grading, one is making a judgement on the whole paper, not even question by question but in terms of overall standard. I am reminded of a flower or vegetable show, in which one can see whether a presentation satisfies the requirements in terms of number, size, freshness, etc., but what counts is an overall impression very hard to define.

I have often heard members of a Grading Committee point to a particularly inspired point made in an answer and say, 'Any candidate with the understanding to make that point deserves grade A', or equally, pointing out some particularly crass blunder, 'Any candidate who can write something as stupid as that doesn't deserve to pass at all.' Yet the two candidates may have the same total mark, or the one with the blunder may perhaps even have the higher mark. Such judgements can never, of course, over-ride the actual mark totals awarded, but they indicate how difficult the required judgement is to make. One flash of brilliance or stupidity has to be set in the context of a complete paper, probably in the main consisting of very routine answers.

One is influenced by almost subliminal factors. If a script is particularly neat, clearly written and well set out one will feel better disposed towards it than towards a scruffy script which is hard to read. An old friend of mine, with long experience as a senior examiner, used to refer to 'the smell of the script'. He felt that in some way which he could not define he was sensing the quality of the candidate. He would sometimes say, 'I should have liked to teach this candidate. This is top-grade work.' But other examiners might have felt quite differently about the same work.

When I was first involved in examining, grading judgements were taken holistically for the syllabus. This required the Grading Committee not merely to consider one component of a candidate's work but to consider the whole of the work. The difficulties described above are at once magnified: it becomes so much harder to find examples of uniform performance; it is so much more likely that here and there in one or other of the components isolated points may arise to influence the examiner contrary to the pointers in the rest of the work. When the Boards began to grade component by component, using mathematical aggregation to combine the separate decisions into a syllabus decision, they at first expected the Grading Committees to agree upon precise boundaries. For the reasons given above this was soon seen to be impossible. Of course precise boundaries were decided, because they had to be, but this would be by majority decision, not unanimously, and could even be influenced by one eloquent and strong personality on the Committee, with the others agreeing in order to catch their trains home. Sometimes it meant that the Principal Examiner for the component gave his view and the others simply went along with him because, being responsible for different components, they had no direct experience of marking the component under discussion. Thus from the mid-'90s the Boards have adopted the realistic principle of 'an area of uncertainty'.

The procedure now requires the team to read those scripts

carrying the mark at the top of the chosen range. If the range has been well chosen there will be unanimity that these scripts deserve the higher grade. The scripts one mark down are then read, and so on until there is disagreement. This identifies the top of the area of uncertainty. The team then moves to the bottom of the range and works upwards in the same way. The process can be represented schematically as shown in Table 4.1.

Table 4.1

Mark	Committee view
72	Clear grade A
71	Uncertain
70	
69	Uncertain
68	Clearly not grade A
67	Clearly not grade A

(The scripts on mark 70 were not read since the area of uncertainty had been identified before they were reached.)

Having established an area of uncertainty the actual grade boundary will be placed at one of those uncertain points using all available evidence, primarily of course the statistical evidence. At this point, scripts which had not been read on any mark, because the area of uncertainty was established before that mark was reached, will be read. It would be quite wrong to allow the possibility of the boundary being placed on a mark at which the scripts had not been considered. It would be natural to expect the decision to fall on the mid-point of the area of uncertainty (70 in this example), but statistical factors or any perceived trend in the strength of the uncertainty, for instance if uncertainty were caused by only one dissenter at one of the extremes but the Committee were equally divided at the other, might lead to the final decision being off-centre.

When the judgemental grade boundaries have been determined in this way (A, B and E for AS and A Level, A, C and F for GCSE) intermediate grade boundaries are inserted mathematically by equal division, and by rounding down to the lower mark, as being more favourable to the candidates, if the division results in a fraction of a mark. The grade below the lowest to be decided judgementally (N for AS and A Level, G for GCSE) is also put in mathematically, using the same band width as the one above, while for GCSE A* is as far above A as B is below it, although in this last case the Grading Committee is allowed some discretion. This may be necessary in a high-scoring syllabus where, if the basic rule were to be followed, it could be possible for A* to require a mark higher than the maximum possible!

AGGREGATING COMPONENT GRADES TO A SYLLABUS GRADE

When the components of the syllabus have been graded, those decisions are carried forward to the syllabus as a whole, the stage at which the result is actually published. At first sight one might expect simple aggregation to be used. If the A-grade boundaries on four components were 75, 72, 73 and 70 what could be more natural than to set 290 as the requirement for grade A in the syllabus? However, at this point one must consider whether one expects a candidate who will be awarded grade A overall to achieve grade A on every component. If so, few A grades would be awarded. Most of the candidates scoring exactly 290, to use the example given, will not actually have achieved grade A on all four components. They will have a few marks above the boundary on one component but a few below on another. So few candidates perform perfectly evenly that probably hardly any with a mark in the 300–290 range will have achieved four A-component grades. On the other hand it is mathematically inevitable that every candidate with a score of 287 will have achieved one A-component grade, and in practice probably most with a score of 280 or better will have done so.

THE 'WEIGHTED AVERAGES' METHOD

The alternative to aggregation is to take into account the percentage of candidates gaining grade A on each component. It is perfectly possible that in the example used above, on each component ten per cent of the candidates might have scored grade A, but that only five per cent will have scored 290, the aggregation of the A marks. This is because some of the candidates who scored grade A on any one component will not have done so on the others. If one chooses the mark at syllabus level which would award grade A to ten per cent of the candidates it will in all probability be well below 290, and perhaps close to 280.

At present the Boards carry out this percentage calculation, averaging out the percentage of candidates achieving grade A at component level (and so too for the other judgemental grades) and allowing for the correct weighting of each component. If one component carries twice the final maximum mark of another it must also be given twice the weight when these percentages are calculated. The mark required at syllabus level to give this percentage outcome is then compared with simple aggregation, and in the best interest of the candidates the lower mark is chosen. The Grading Committee has discretion to choose a mark higher than the lower of these two marks if it has strong reason to do so. This is quite likely in low-entry subjects where figures calculated on the percentage method can be absurd and can vary wildly from year to year. But in a subject with a substantial entry and a normal distribution of ability across the mark range the system works well.

While it is true that at the top grade the percentage method usually gives a lower syllabus mark than that achieved by aggregation, it is equally true that for the bottom grade the reverse occurs. Just as few candidates score a top grade on every component, so very few score a bottom grade uniformly. In this case, when the two calculations are compared the figure given by aggregation will be chosen. If it were not so it would be possible for a candidate to score grade E, for example, on every component but not to be awarded that grade for the syllabus – a manifest absurdity.

THE CONSEQUENCES OF DIFFERENT METHODS

Since the syllabus boundary marks are chosen by selecting the figure which favours the candidates at each grade level, it follows that normally one method is used for grade A and the other for grade E (F in the case of GCSE). For the intermediate decision it may be either, depending upon the distribution of the candidates' marks across the range and the point at which aggregation becomes more favourable. A consequence of this, it may be argued, is that the better the grade the easier it is to gain. A candidate may be awarded grade A while falling well short of grade A aggregation. The leeway allowed will be less for grade B, very little if any for grade C, and in all probability none at all for grades below that. Some candidates, if their performance is fairly even across all components, will be awarded grade A without scoring a single grade A at component level. On the other hand, any candidate who falls short of the lowest grade on any component must gain enough marks above the boundary on another to compensate for the deficiency.

Before the percentage method was introduced, Grading Committees had to place the syllabus boundaries, having agreed component boundaries, using their best judgement, heavily influenced by the statistical outcome generated. My own belief is that for grade A few would have ventured to drop as far below the aggregation mark as the percentage method now enables them to do. My own approach used to be to suggest to Grading Committees that they should drop a number of marks below aggregation one fewer than the number of components. Thus in a four-component syllabus the boundary would be placed three marks below that suggested by aggregation, in a six-component syllabus five marks below, and so on. This guaranteed by mathematical necessity that every candidate awarded the grade would have achieved it on at least one component. Moreover, I should have expected this to be done for every grade boundary, to give absolutely equal treatment to all the candidates across the range.

The introduction of the percentage method is, I am sure, a factor in the apparent improvement of results in the top grades, although of course this will not be a continuing factor. Its effect will have occurred only once, at the point when it was introduced, in the early days of GCSE but much more recently for AS and A Level.

GRADING MODULAR SYLLABUSES

Modular syllabuses introduce a grading problem of their own. For any module the candidates taking it are not a homogeneous group. Some will be taking it with the intention of banking the result and using it for aggregation later; others will be taking it at the session in which they wish the syllabus grade to be awarded. Some of these may be taking it for the second time (or even more), and in some of these cases the result will be worse than that achieved earlier and so will be rejected. For these reasons one cannot use the percentage method for aggregation with any confidence: it would not be clear what such a figure represented. Thus, for modular syllabuses, the marks are converted to the Uniform Mark Scale, described in the previous chapter, and syllabus grading is by aggregation alone – the candidates have no concessions. The impact of modular syllabuses on standards as a whole will be discussed in the next chapter. Many think that they are a factor likely to lower standards, but in this point at least they could be held to be demanding a higher standard than that required of those following the linear route.

A FINAL CHECK

When the procedures described above have been completed, one final stage remains. The Code of Practice places responsibility for ensuring the quality and standards of its qualifications upon a single named person, normally the Chief Executive, in the Board. The Chief Executive or nominated deputy must therefore have a mechanism in place whereby this responsibility can be exercised. The Grading Committees cannot be allowed to take decisions without having to report and justify them. In the Board with which I am myself most familiar there is a Grading Advisory Committee (GAC) which meets with the Chair of Examiners and Subject Officer shortly after the Grading Meeting. The Chief Executive or his deputy will be supported by statistical experts and will study the data in minute detail. They will have before them both the same data which the Grading Committee had, and also the data generated by its decisions, i.e. the percentages of candidates awarded each grade. They will require any apparent anomalies to be explained and justified.

The GAC may require the original Grading Committee to be reconvened and to reconsider its decisions. However, in view of the very tight time constraints at this stage of the process, if they are really unhappy they are more likely to persuade the Chair of Examiners to implement by chairman's authority an adjustment to the grade boundaries which his Committee had agreed.

From this it will appear that statistical considerations, viewed by people with no specific subject understanding, may be allowed to over-ride the professional judgements of a committee of subject specialists. This is true, and its validity has to be debatable, but in practice it is rare. The great justification of the system is that the Grading Committee, knowing that it must clear this hurdle, will have taken its decisions with the greatest possible care, and when it can see for itself that they may be challenged it will have satisfied itself that it has a convincing justification. Armed with this justification the Chair of Examiners will face the Grading Advisory Committee with equanimity, and will expect to be able to persuade them that the original decisions were entirely correct. The Chief Executive will in turn leave the meeting armed with powerful justification for what has been agreed if in turn the regulatory body is tempted to query the statistics.

The object is to keep professional judgement and statistical considerations in balance, not allowing either to over-rule the other. At the completion of this complex process it is hard to see what else could be done to ensure the correct grading decisions.

Chapter 5

Standards – What Are They and How Are They Maintained?

Every summer, when the GCSE and A-Level results are published, the press – and often politicians too – have a great deal to say about standards: they have fallen, or even been shamefully diluted, or they have risen and are a credit to pupils and teachers alike, according to the axe the particular writer has to grind. So how might one assess the truth? What evidence is there and how can it be interpreted? This chapter aims to tackle this issue in detail.

THE IMPORTANCE OF JUDGEMENT

The previous two chapters have laid great stress on the importance of professional judgement in the examining process. There is no way of demonstrating that standards determined in this way could ever be maintained with absolute certainty. When I am asked if examination standards have risen or fallen I reply by asking if standards in ice skating have risen or fallen. Judgement in the two activities seems to me to be surprisingly comparable. When a skater has performed, a group of judges each individually award a mark. No doubt there are measurable details to which they can point; for instance the number and variety of jumps and spins can be counted, and the fact of a skater falling is indisputable. But artistic impression has its own separate mark, equal to the mark for technical merit, and the very use of the word 'impression' makes my point.

Ice-skating judges mark out of six and use decimal points. This is in effect the same as marking out of 60. Perhaps television only shows the good performances, but I do not recall ever seeing a score below 4.8, and even that was exceptional. In effect these judges have a spread of scarcely ten marks whereby to discriminate between the skaters. Even so, it is not unusual to see a divergence of three or four points, say from 5.5 to 5.8, between judges marking the same performance. In GCSE and A-Level examining a discrepancy of three marks between examiners on a scale of 0 to 60 would be regarded with concern, while if the effective range were only ten marks, such a discrepancy would be totally unacceptable. The results would be little more than a lottery – which examiner happened to have marked the work of a particular candidate – and someone would be liable for dismissal. The Examining Boards simply would not have the possibility of solving the problem as ice skating does by having a whole team of markers to mark the work of every candidate and aggregating the marks, to iron out differences of opinion between markers.

It would be an interesting exercise to ask ice-skating judges to view videos of performances from years gone by and to mark them according to present criteria. This ought to tell us if standards have changed, but even so it would be difficult to separate the skater's performance from changed presentational possibilities. If today's materials and techniques make it possible to produce more elegant, attractive, convenient costumes, if modern acoustic facilities have created better musical accompaniment, if modern lighting techniques have enabled the skater to make a more striking visual impact, the mark for artistic impression is bound to go up, even if she is not in the smallest degree a better skater. Every performance, whether by a skater or an examination candidate, takes place in a context. Comparison over time demands comparison of the changing contexts.

THE CONTEXT IN WHICH A SUBJECT IS STUDIED

I am sure that in education no single answer can be given to the question of whether standards have changed. I am sure that in some subjects the standard is lower than it was 40 years ago, that in others it is higher, and that in others changes in the nature of the syllabuses have been so great that direct comparison is impossible. But every change, whether for easier or for harder, will have taken place for a reason, within a context, and is fully explicable. The real question should be, 'Is the standard appropriate?'

To begin with my own personal experience, I studied the Classics (Latin, Greek and Ancient History) for A Level, taken in 1953. I have no doubt at all that in the Latin and Greek languages I was far ahead of the standard required today; I had read far more of the writings of the classical authors, the texts prescribed for the examinations were longer, we undertook much more complex exercises in details of grammatical and syntactical obscurity. By A Level I was quite possibly as advanced as many graduates in those languages today. However, from the age of 13 I read no Science of any kind, no History, no Geography. My O-Level range, excluding my specialist subjects, was English (both Language and Literature), Mathematics, French and Religious Studies. I am less well educated in a general sense than those who study Classics today, even if I was a more advanced classicist. I very much regret the gaps in my education, and if I had the choice I should prefer to have been educated on a modern curriculum.

To be fair to my specialist subjects, before moving on to discuss those more central to the curriculum, I ought to add that the study of Latin and Greek has changed since I was a student. Then it was first and foremost a study of language; no technical detail was too obscure to be ignored. Today it is a study of literature; no student will achieve a good examination result without a talent for literary criticism and literary appreciation, and moreover without a grasp of the social, historical and political context in which the literature was produced. These were aspects of the subject of which I was scarcely aware when I took A Level. So even my claim of the previous paragraph to have been a more advanced classicist than those who study it today may be unjustified. We are not comparing like with like; it is a matter of opinion which aspect of the work is more demanding – and more worthy of study. What is essential is to agree on those skills which it is important for our young people to acquire, and to pursue them to the highest standard possible. If this means reducing the attention to other skills which were more central in the past, so be it.

THE SCIENCES

The most dramatic change has probably been in the Sciences. I am told that an A-Level candidate in Science today will have the knowledge required to make a nuclear bomb (mercifully, he will not have the resources!). I wonder if any of those who argue today that educational standards are not what they were could have made the same claim. The expansion of scientific knowledge has been so great and so rapid that a specialist of 40 years ago would struggle to understand an A-Level question paper today, let alone to answer it.

Why is it then that universities today claim that students joining them to follow a course in the Sciences are less well prepared than they were? Why do they argue that they need an extra year on the university course? The answer must lie in this same explosion of scientific knowledge. If scientific knowledge has doubled in the last 40 years (a speculative figure picked at random to exemplify the argument; it might even have trebled) an A-Level student could be further down the track than her predecessor but still not as close to the finishing line. If I train for the 5,000 metres but then find I am entered for the 10,000 metres I might need rather more training before I can run it. The need for an extra year of university study is nothing to do with any change in the standard of A-Level courses. If A-Level courses in Science were now what they were 40 years ago, universities would be clamouring for an extra two years on the course.

MODERN LANGUAGES

Modern Languages have changed rather differently. In the past they were fundamentally a literary study. The caricature of the university professor who knew everything to be known about the writings of Maupassant or Voltaire but who could not buy what he wanted in a French shop was no doubt unfair, but nevertheless reflected a truth: Modern Languages were for studying, not for speaking. Nowadays languages are studied first and foremost as a means of communication – spoken or written – in real, plausible, contemporary contexts. As a country we have a pathetic reputation as linguists – primarily, I believe, because languages were given the wrong focus in the way in which they were taught. Today's students will know less about literature (some A-Level courses demand no study of literature at all, which may be a step too far in the other direction) but should be able to cope confidently and easily when required to use the language.

So have standards in Modern Languages dropped compared with the past? Again it is a question of the type, 'Is this apple better than this pear?' They are different, even if similar. It is more realistic to ask, 'Which is more useful? Which is more worthy of study?' Having chosen the appropriate syllabus we must of course press for it to be taught as well as possible, and for the Examining Boards to demand a proper standard and to allow no soft options in it. But the former syllabus in itself is not the proper yardstick.

HISTORY AND RELATED SUBJECTS

There is also a range of syllabuses, of which History is a prime example, where there used to be a major focus upon factual knowledge but where this emphasis has changed. The British are very much of the 'Mastermind mentality', where the ability to produce on the instant any obscure factual detail is highly valued: the popularity of quiz games on radio and television and of pub quiz leagues demonstrates that. Once upon a time learning History meant learning names and dates; but to be able to list Henry VIII's wives in the correct order is no more the mark of a historian than to be able to list the moons of Jupiter. A historian must be able to understand, to explain causes and consequences, to evaluate; to be able to weigh evidence, allowing for bias, propaganda and simple error in the sources; to be able to prove the facts, not merely to know them. This is where the emphasis is now being placed in the teaching, and therefore in the examining, of History. A consequence is that if students are to study History in much greater depth they will not be able to cover the same breadth. The critical way of making this point, if one wants to be cynical, is to say that they will know more and more about less and less. Those who write and approve syllabuses must ensure that a proper balance is struck, and I am very confident that they do. But neither the GCSE nor the A-Level course must be seen in isolation. Schoolchildren from the early days of their education learn History. By the time they embark on an examination course they should have gained a broad perspective of historical events and be aware of the focal points. The examination courses are designed to add historical skills to an existing framework of factual knowledge.

MATHEMATICS

The two key subjects are of course English and Mathematics. These are the two which everyone takes for GCSE, and these are the two which have attracted the most charges of falling standards. We are very used to hearing statements that young people today cannot spell, cannot construct proper sentences, cannot do simple arithmetical calculations. If, despite these perceived weaknesses, they are the holders of acceptable GCSE and A-Level grades the inference is that these examinations have allowed their standards to collapse. I certainly do not deny the importance of these basic skills and am totally certain that they must be inculcated into young people at some stage of their education. But if examinations have moved those skills out of focus, something else will now be in focus instead. Examinations do not examine and reward nothing. So what has now taken centre stage? How important is it?

Like Science, Mathematics has made great strides in recent years. The development of the SMP and MEI syllabuses has introduced concepts new to examining at age 16 and 18. Similarly the availability of the calculator has made it possible to set in examinations questions which could not have been set before, because they could not have been done in the time available by longhand methods. This in one sense is a real raising of standards. But if calculators can be used, longhand methods will tend to be neglected. This is almost inevitably regarded as a bad thing by older generations who were brought up on longhand methods and pride themselves on their facility in, say, mental arithmetic. I wonder if there were similar feelings about young people losing their skill with the abacus when it was superseded? I expect so. What we must do is identify how far old skills are still needed, teach them thoroughly (and examine them too) if they are required, but abandon them unhesitatingly if they are not.

It seems to me that what is still required is what might be called 'civic arithmetic'. By this I mean the ability to check one's bill in the supermarket, to check one's tax return, to do simple calculations involved in a DIY job. If you are one of those who believe that standards in Mathematics have fallen, stop and think of the circumstances in which you have found this to be true. I feel sure it will be in the sorts of situation that I have suggested above. Arithmetic and Mathematics are not identical, although at least before the availability of the calculator one could hardly cope with the latter without the former. Arithmetic is what one learns in the early years of education; it should be mastered before the GCSE course proper begins. Much of what one studies in Mathematics involves concepts not in immediate everyday use, not so visible to those who criticize modern standards. Basic ability in arithmetic, a highly desirable skill, must be inculcated as early as possible, and accredited in Key Stage examinations prior to GCSE.

I am sure that attempts to tamper with GCSE and A-Level

Mathematics syllabuses in order to throw emphasis back onto arithmetic is a mistake. It cannot be done without losing something from the strengths of modern syllabuses. In particular I am sceptical about any move to make a part of the A-Level examination calculator-free. Questions to be tackled without the aid of a calculator will have to be fairly straightforward to be answerable in the time available; probably fewer questions will have to be required in the time. This may lead to an improvement in arithmetical skills, but only at the expense of higher mathematical skills. Nor do I think that A-Level candidates are the right target. They will be studying Mathematics at A Level because they were very good at it at GCSE. If they make arithmetical slips, as they do, it will be because of haste, not of inability. We all make slips in things at which we are normally very good. I simply do not believe that A-Level mathematicians are incapable of accurate mathematical calculation on a regular basis. I equally believe that the demands of the Mathematics (not Arithmetic) syllabuses are greater than they were 40 years ago.

ENGLISH

English generates its own problems. It is true that this is a subject in which the body of knowledge has not increased, as is the case with Science and Mathematics. Yes, new novels, plays and poems are constantly being published, some of which are deservedly added to examination syllabuses – but the essence of what candidates have to do is unchanged. I suspect that there has been a greater continuity of examination demand in English than in almost any other subject. I have every confidence that examiners expect as much as, and probably more than, they did years ago in terms of critical and appreciative response to literature, in terms of ability to construct and sustain an argument, in terms of personal response and imaginative writing. The charge of falling standards focuses upon two charges, the first of which concerns the open-book approach to examinations.

In a number of subjects candidates nowadays are allowed to take textbooks into the examination room. This is normally the case when literature is involved and arises in Modern Languages as well as English. Critics take it for granted that if the candidate has the text available, the examination must be easy. In fact the availability of the text simply enables the examiners to ask more searching questions. Instead of asking the candidate to remember the story, for which purpose the candidate will have spent interminable hours mugging up every last detail in case it comes up in the examination paper, the examiners can require the candidate to think more conceptually and to write sophisticated critical analysis for which reference to the text will be extremely beneficial. Clearly the candidate is not freed from the need to have a good working knowledge of the text, since the more familiar he is with it the more quickly he will be able to find the passages useful to answer the question in the examination room, and to some extent he will also find it less necessary to check up on passages with which he is already familiar. But the presence of the text, so far from making the examination easier, enables the examiners to test skills of a higher order than they might otherwise feel able to do.

So far as I know, no examination allows texts to be taken into the examination for every component. A well-constructed examination will cover a range of skills, demanding unaided memory in some papers but allowing access to data in others. In the traditional examination the lack of reference data is a feature almost never replicated in the rest of one's life. In any other situation, if I do not know something or cannot remember it, I can look it up. Subject experts at the highest level have reference material at their elbow as they work, and feel no shame about referring to it as necessary. When I visit my doctor I expect him, of course, to be sufficiently expert to consider my case without constant reference to medical books, but I should prefer him to check on anything about which he was unsure, and I should think none the worse of him for so doing. Only the unfortunate examination candidate is put into the position of being deprived of any forms of reference and having to work entirely from memory. When there are components in an examination which change this approach it is not only more natural but also adds greater freedom and range to the testing, making for a more valid result.

The second and more serious charge focuses upon spelling, punctuation and grammar. As with Mathematics we are dealing with fundamentals best inculcated in the early stages of education. Here too the basics should be taught and assessed in the Key Stage examinations prior to GCSE. However, unlike Mathematics, these basic requirements pervade the GCSE and A-Level examinations, and not only in English but in every subject which requires continuous written responses. When there are failings they are visible for all to see, and can lead to a feeling that good grades should not be awarded, even when the assessment objectives of the subject have been well met in all other respects.

I recall some years ago being challenged on this issue of spelling by a lady active in local government and a school governor. She told me that her nephew had recently shown her his doctoral thesis in some obscure aspect of Physics. She had begun to read it, but after one page had thrust it aside, declaring that if she had been the examiner she would have failed it without hesitation because the spelling was so bad. In other words – but she would not have put it this way herself – a good physicist, possibly one who would contribute in research, or industry or teaching to the welfare of mankind, would have been prevented from moving ahead in his career simply because he could not spell. One must keep the issues in perspective.

However, I have to agree that in this respect standards in English *have* fallen. Because of television, many young people read less than they used to do; because of the telephone they no longer write letters; dating from the '60s there was a long period when teachers neglected spelling, punctuation and grammar, arguing that it was more important for children to write imaginatively without the need to worry about technicalities. Our society itself tends to encourage unorthodox spelling; when a supermarket calls itself Kwiksave a signal is being given, and one could cite hundreds of similar examples. Nowadays, if a piece of writing is important, it is easy to produce it on a word processor and to use a spellcheck.

Regarding English, then, I see no evidence that standards have fallen, except in these technical aspects discussed. Very probably they have risen. In awarding grades in English itself these aspects must be one part of the assessment objectives, and therefore must have their impact upon the grades awarded. A separate award specifically in Use of English might well be a useful addition to the range of qualifications available. There used to be such an award taken in parallel with A Level, but the Boards abandoned it because the number of candidates taking it became so small: no users – universities or employers – seemed to be interested in it. Perhaps there is again a need for it. A candidate with grade A in English but grade E in Use of English (or perhaps a better title could be found) would be identifiable as someone with plenty of well-expressed, well-ordered ideas but little ability to spell them or to punctuate them. Users would know where they stood.

NATURAL EXPECTATION

If perceived weaknesses in numeracy and spelling are a root cause of the belief that examination standards have been allowed to slip, another is disbelief that standards can rise at the rate that increasing awards of top grades suggest that they are now doing. This is a gut feeling on the part of educational commentators: if twice as many candidates are awarded grades A to C as there used to be, the Boards must be giving these grades away like Smarties. Those of us from older generations find it very hard to accept that the modern generation may be brighter than we were.

For any given subject only experts in that subject can give an authoritative answer, and I have indicated already that one is rarely comparing like with like because of changes to syllabuses over time. Let us look at other non-subject-specific pointers.

In most aspects of human activity there is progress over time, sometimes rapid and widespread. In any athletic event the number of young people who can run a given distance in a given time, or jump or throw a given distance, has increased steadily. Why should this not be true in the academic field? In both there have been improvements in facilities and support which would naturally lead to improvements in performance. In preparation for examinations the Boards now give help which was never given until the last ten years or so: regular INSET for teachers, syllabuses which spell out the assessment objectives and how they will be weighted, publication of mark-schemes. Teachers have a range of educational visits and teaching materials, including the use of computers, which can add a new dimension to their teaching. Moreover, the pressure on pupils to do well has become almost excessive, but must be having its effect. Thirty or forty years ago examination results had a very low profile (all the attention was being given to the rights and wrongs of 11+) and many students did not take what was then O Level. Today GCSE seems to be the only focus of attention for everyone from the age of about 13.

From time to time the Government issues educational attainment targets, indicating how many 16-year-olds it expects to achieve grades A to C in five GCSE subjects and two A-Level passes. These figures are so far ahead of what is currently achieved that if the rate of increase needed to meet them were seen in the published examination results, credibility would indeed be stretched. Yet when successive Governments evolve educational policies specifically designed to make these targets possible, I find it quite astonishing that Government Ministers are so often in the forefront of those decrying the examination results. One would expect them to take a lead in acclaiming those results as proof that their own policy is working. I wonder if public disbelief in improving examination results is based upon nothing more than disbelief that any Government policy could actually work!

DIFFERENT TYPES OF SUBJECT

A further factor which leads to scepticism about examination achievement is the introduction of new subjects, which traditionalists find it hard to accept as valid examination subjects. Examples include Media Studies, Sports Studies and Social Studies, while a generation brought up on Economics will look with doubt upon the growth of Business Studies at the expense of Economics, and traditional classicists may raise an eyebrow when they see Classical Civilisation replacing the study of Latin and Greek in many schools. Are there in reality two categories of subject, the truly academic forming a sort of premier league, and a second division of soft options?

In my own mind there are indeed two categories of subject, but I should like to divide them differently, and the division does not necessarily imply a difference in standard. My division is into those subjects in which a reasonably educated and intelligent person could attempt the examination without having followed a course of study, and those for which a course of study is necessary even to understand the question paper, let alone to answer it. In the latter category most obviously come languages, Science and Mathematics. On the other hand most of us could read the question paper in English, Social Studies, perhaps Twentieth-century History and many others, think of something to say and so produce a plausible, if sketchy, answer. We should not be well supplied with facts, we should not know of alternative theories and findings. Nor should we know that we did not know these things, and therefore we should have a higher opinion of our answer than it deserved, and a correspondingly low opinion of the demands of the subject. A fair judgement requires attention to the assessment objectives of the subject and an awareness of how much study is required to meet those objectives. Every subject must have a body of facts to be learned, concepts to be understood, skills to be applied. I think that the varying credibility given to different subjects derives more from traditional prejudices than from reality. Of course easy syllabuses and examination papers could be set. It is the function of the quality controls within the Boards, and the supervisory bodies described elsewhere in this book, to ensure that this does not happen. Criticism should only be offered when based upon in-depth analysis, not upon superficial prejudice.

THE IMPACT OF COURSEWORK

The examinations have also attracted criticism because of the role of coursework. To a traditionalist an examination is taken under close supervision, with a strict time limit, in an examination room. Work done in the candidate's own time must be suspect: the candidates will cheat; parents or friends will do the work for them; the teachers will connive at it. Of course there is scope for malpractice in coursework (as there is too in traditional examinations), but there is no evidence that this is a real problem, while the value of coursework is important, particularly in some subjects.

To put it at its lowest, it helps to modify the fact that an examination grade depends upon a particular performance upon a particular day. More seriously, it enables some subjects to be examined properly, as they could not be without it. Sciences demand practical examinations, art and craft subjects require work which has to be produced over time, History and similar subjects properly involve research skills which could not be tested in an examination room. This has often added an extra dimension to a subject; so far from making it easier it has added something else for the candidate to tackle, an additional skill to be developed. It is often time-consuming, and indeed a major problem to GCSE candidates with coursework deadlines to be met at about the same time in six, seven, even eight subjects. I am quite certain that when taken seriously, as it must be if good marks are to be gained, it is never easy. On the other hand candidates frequently become absorbed by it and enjoy it. If enjoying work makes it easier then on that ground, and on that ground only, coursework is an easy option.

THE IMPACT OF MODULAR SYLLABUSES

Traditionalists also challenge the spread, now I am sure unstoppable, of modular syllabuses. To be able to take a syllabus a stage at a time, to be examined on that stage and put it aside as one moves on to the next, and even to be able to take it again if one has not done well enough, must make the examination easier. In only one respect do I believe this to be true: for any modular examination only the material covered by that module has to be familiar, whereas in a traditional linear syllabus, with all the examination papers falling within the space of perhaps ten days, all the material has to be retained, revised and familiar together at the end of the course.

For this reason the powers that be are now requiring the Boards to introduce a 'synoptic' element into any modular syllabus. How this will work out remains to be seen, but in many subjects I believe that it will be totally artificial and will create serious difficulties for all concerned, not least the candidates. The alleged problem is that, whereas in a linear syllabus the candidate is required to have a complete grasp of all the material in the syllabus over the period of the actual examination, at no point in the modular course does the candidate have a complete grasp of all the material; by the time the last module is taken the content of the first may have been forgotten. The proposed solution is to have a module which draws together the material of the whole syllabus.

Whatever the rights and wrongs of this, in most linear syllabuses there is no component which draws together all the material in this way. A candidate in English may write a paper on Shakespeare on one day and twentieth-century novels the next, without having to cope with questions bringing the two together. In this example it could of course be done: questions seeking to compare Shakespearean attitudes, characterization, use of language, etc. with those of the twentieth century are possible. But in many subjects – not least, I suspect, in Mathematics and Science, which first pioneered modular syllabuses – I feel sure that there are areas of content which are clearly separate and cannot be brought together into a synoptic view. Some subjects, of which History is a striking example, are defined not by content but by skills. It does not matter whether a candidate chooses to study modern or medieval history. The course must cover both British and non-British material, but these need not coincide in date. Since across the whole candidature the material studied will cover virtually the whole span of world history, it is hard to see how a question could be put before all the candidates which all would be equally able to tackle. Any such question would have to be a test of historical skills, with the candidate free to use whatever factual content she knew. But if this were so the paper would have no more synoptic force than any other module, since it is in terms of skills, not of content, that the assessment objectives for the subject are defined and every one of the modules is assessed.

To be fair to the policy-makers, I must add that it is the intention to introduce this sort of synoptic element into linear syllabuses also. However, when it is introduced I believe that it will either be fudged in some way, or that syllabuses will not only become harder than they are at present but also than their traditional linear predecessors, which were the yardstick by which the standard of modular syllabuses was to be measured. If in fact the existing structure has made them easier, I believe that the way in which modular marks are aggregated to give syllabus grades, described in Chapter 3, more than offsets any advantage.

Of course the possibility of a re-sit of an individual module may be of advantage to the candidate. It should make the results appear better from a statistical point of view, since candidates will not cash in poor results but will wait until a re-sit gives a better outcome. If poor candidates exclude themselves from the published results it will appear superficially as if the results are better than they really are. But to an individual candidate a re-sit is never easy. If a school is to teach six modules over the two years of the course it is likely to teach one module per term (roughly speaking; terms are of course of slightly different lengths, and the sixth is only about half a term because of the final examination). A candidate wishing to take a re-sit will have to prepare for it in a class studying for the next module, while at the same time also studying for that module along with the others. It is by no means uncommon to find a candidate performing worse at the second time of asking, for this reason.

WHAT IS THE 'RIGHT' STANDARD?

It is also worth asking those who claim that standards have fallen whether they are justified in assuming that the former 'higher' standards were right. A major change in the approach to examining has been a switch from negative to positive marking. It was possible for the former to result in candidates not gaining credit for what they knew, understood and could do. A particularly striking example used to arise in the case of dictation in Modern Languages (a skill, incidentally, no longer tested). One mark was deducted for each mistake, so that if a passage were 100 words long and 20 marks were available a candidate who got 80 words right would score no marks, since the 20 words wrong would have cost all the marks. Nowadays in a test of that nature the proportion of the material correct would lead to that proportion of the marks being awarded.

Similarly in my own subject, Latin, it used to be the case when I was first an examiner that candidates who omitted a word in translation could be penalized up to three marks, being deemed to have failed not only in their knowledge of the meaning of the word but also in its grammatical features, of which there were probably at least two. But a candidate who guessed a wrong meaning and correctly showed the grammatical elements would lose only one mark. Since Examining Boards at that time did not publish their mark-schemes, as they now do, candidates did not know of this severity (unless their teacher also happened to be an examiner, able to instruct them in examination technique). The candidate who left the gap might well have been able to handle the grammar, but did not know that it was worth guessing a meaning.

I suspect that similar examples of penal marking could have been found in most subjects. One consequence was that some candidates did not get the grades which they deserved – and schools did not challenge results in those days as they do now. Alternatively – or additionally – grade boundaries had to be set lower than one would expect to compensate for this harsh marking down of the candidates. Results today may well be much more realistic and may much more accurately reflect the quality of the candidates.

COMPARATIVE STANDARDS BETWEEN BOARDS

If the issue of standards over time is the one which most captures public attention, that of comparative standards between Boards is more important. Candidates in different years are not in direct competition with one another, let alone candidates from different generations; candidates in the same year are most definitely in competition. In years gone by minimal effort was made to establish consistency across Boards; today all that can be done is done. First, all syllabuses have to be written to satisfy criteria agreed jointly between the Boards themselves and the Qualifications and Curriculum Authority (QCA). Two syllabuses in the same subject will certainly satisfy the same criteria. Second, all syllabuses have to be approved by the QCA. This approval also involves the approval of a set of specimen question papers, together with their mark-schemes. If these are not setting the correct standard, the syllabus, however satisfactory it may be in itself, will not be approved, since the examiners responsible for it have not demonstrated that they can examine it appropriately. Third, the QCA conducts a regular series of scrutinies, sending in observers to watch all the processes of the examination, from setting the question papers through to grading the results. Its primary objective is to keep the Boards in line, and its reports sometimes record a view that a Board's results are slightly out of line, coupled with an instruction to take appropriate action in future. (It could presumably refuse to validate a set of results, although in practice it must be highly improbable that it would ever do so. On the one hand this would leave a set of candidates without a result, for no fault of their own; on the other it could hardly be done in time to prevent the publication of the original results, since the production of the scrutineers' report takes some time, involving the amalgamation of the views of different scrutineers, each of whom has observed different parts of the process.)

Despite this detailed care we are clearly back in the realm of professional judgement. Even with common criteria there is no way of proving that two syllabuses will be equally demanding when they are actually examined. Scrutineers report on what has happened and give guidance for the future, but even so the next examination paper will be a different one, while inevitably the senior examining personnel will also change from time to time. So can statistical evidence be of help?

If statistics are to be used, much more detailed analysis will be necessary than has ever been undertaken. My own experience when working for the Oxford and Cambridge Schools Examination Board (OCSEB) illustrates this. We were often accused of being too generous because statistically we gave substantially more top grades than any other Board. If we gave, say, twenty per cent of the candidates grade A, others were probably giving about ten per cent. On the other hand schools themselves took the view that we were too difficult, and many chose other Boards for that reason. Were we setting hard papers, and so deterring schools from taking our examinations, but over-compensating when it came to the grading, and so giving the impression of generosity? Our own argument (naturally!) was that we attracted the most able candidates and that all was well at all points. Eventually our research department undertook an analysis of the results of ourselves and the other Boards by centre type. The very large majority of the OCSEB candidates came from the independent sector, including some of the most academically prestigious schools in the country. When we isolated the results of this category of candidates we found that in comparison with other Boards we were, if anything, slightly severe. Thus, although another Board might have only been awarding grade A to ten per cent of its candidates, it might well have been awarding that grade to 25 per cent or more of its candidates from independent schools.

Each Board has its own traditional clientele. In a large-entry subject one would expect the statistics to be roughly parallel, especially since the recent merging of Boards has ironed out the more marked differences in their respective candidatures. Whether one should expect there to be differences between a Board examining primarily in the south-east and another examining primarily in the north it would be foolhardy to speculate. But it would be equally bold to assert that there is no difference. Only a striking anomaly in the statistics might suggest anything wrong, and thankfully there is no evidence in present statistics sufficient to lead to any suspicion that one Board is easier than another.

JUDGING THE COMPARATIVE DIFFICULTY OF DIFFERENT SUBJECTS

Much more intractable is the issue of different standards between subjects, about which a little has already been said with reference to the introduction of new subjects, which some critics do not accept as having the validity of those from the more traditional curriculum. But even among the traditional subjects there are some which have a reputation for difficulty. Physics is a striking example. Is it in fact harder than, say, French, or even than other Sciences such as Chemistry? How might one find out?

The evidence of the results actually obtained proves nothing. If one took raw results alone one would be led to infer that the easiest subjects of all are Greek and Russian! This is because they attract a highly select entry; virtually no candidates fail, or even drop below grade C, because such candidates do not opt for these subjects in the first place. On the other hand there are easily accessible subjects for which the actual results would suggest that they are very difficult. This is because such subjects are chosen by candidates struggling to find something which they can actually attempt, candidates who may scarcely be of examination standard at all. Some better form of analysis is required.

All Boards accordingly use subject-pairs analysis to give them more meaningful pointers. The theory is that if, say, 100 candidates were to take the same two subjects, the results in those subjects ought to be roughly the same. Those who did better in one subject would be counterbalanced by those who did better in the other. The problem is to have sufficient candidates in the pair to give statistical significance. For GCSE the number of candidates is quite large and one could expect such an analysis to be meaningful; at A Level the analysis may be possible for related subjects but is unlikely otherwise. For instance, to stay with the comparisons of Physics with French and Chemistry, so few candidates at A Level take both Physics and French that statistics will not be meaningful, whereas probably sufficient take both Physics and Chemistry for the figures to tell us something.

So far as I am aware analysis of this kind has not yet been given close attention, nor do I know of any clear understanding of the number of candidates necessary before the analysis becomes significant. Nowadays so many candidates spread their entries across different Boards that candidates in Physics with one Board may well be taking Chemistry with another. There has certainly been no subject-pairs analysis attempted at a national level, and at present the computer systems are not in place to do it.

Obviously subject-pairs analysis cannot be carried out until all the grading has been completed. Inevitably it reports on what has happened too late for any adjustments to be made for the results being analysed. What happens, in my experience, is that the results of this analysis are reported to Subject Committees when they hold their post-mortem meetings. They may then note that in respect of closely related subjects they are severe (or lenient) and may ask for this fact to be brought to the attention of the Grading Committee for the next session of examining. In all probability, however, there will be conflicting evidence. If Chemistry turns out to be lenient in relation to Physics but severe in relation to Mathematics, what are its examiners to do? They will in all probability do nothing, leaving it to the other two subjects to adjust suitably. But Physics and Mathematics may themselves be faced with conflicting pointers (obviously other subjects will be generating information too, not merely those which I am suggesting by way of example). The outcome will be that adjustments, if any, will be minimal and each separate Subject Committee will conclude that its standards are about right.

DO SUBJECT DIFFERENCES MATTER?

In fact I suspect that it is in comparison between subjects that discrepancies are most likely to lie. I believe Physics to be substantially harder than Media Studies, but I know that this has not been proved, and it may be that there is not sufficient evidence to prove it. Does it matter? The standards applied in every subject at both GCSE and A Level are part of a continuum in that subject, from the point at which it begins to be learned (in the case of English one might even argue that it begins at birth) to university degree level. If one adjusted a subject at any point in the continuum, one would also have to adjust elsewhere. A change at GCSE would move the starting point for A Level, and might also change the end point for A Level, if the original end point could no longer be reached or could now clearly be surpassed. A change at A Level would have a similar effect on the university course. Is it worth disrupting the continuum in one subject because it is out of line with another? How important would it be to a physicist if Media Studies were proved to be easier? To the physicist himself Media Studies, however easy in broad statistical terms, might be quite hard. The candidate with the turn of mind to cope with Physics might have no aptitude at all for a subject testing quite different skills, as Media Studies does. I myself found Latin no problem, but my artistic skills were abysmal. If someone had produced evidence that Art was two or three grades easier than Latin (purely for example; I am not suggesting that it is) I should not have given up Latin and switched to Art.

My belief is that related subjects are reasonably in line. It is only in related subjects that evidence can be found which is sufficient to be plausible, and if there were any striking differences they would have been found and dealt with. Moreover, it is only the comparison between related subjects which matters, at least at A Level, because it is only between related subjects that candidates choose. A candidate may choose three of Double Mathematics (counting as two), Physics, Chemistry and Biology, or three of English, History, Classical Civilization, Sociology and French. He is unlikely to pick a mix from both groups. Even so, it would be a good thing if more work were to be done on this aspect of comparative standards. However, if it were done, it would still be necessary to exercise a measure of professional judgement to determine the true meaning of the statistics.

The message of this chapter has been that all issues of standards are a matter of professional judgement, and that in each separate subject those with the necessary expertise are satisfied that the standards currently set are appropriate in their full context, that they fit properly within the present continuum, in the light of the teaching time available to them, and that they lead properly into the next level of study.

Chapter 6

Quality Controls

In any industry – and examining is a form of industry – quality controls are necessary. However carefully planned the processes may be, they are in the hands of fallible human beings. Disappointed candidates will always be convinced that the grade awarded must be wrong. How likely is this, and what can be done about it?

CLERICAL CHECKS

Before the results are issued, the Board will have applied two safety nets: clerical check and grade review. The former is itself in two stages. First, the examiner is required to employ a checker (any responsible adult can be chosen, but it is most commonly husband or wife) who will be paid to check every script after it has been marked. The checker must verify that every answer on the script has been marked, that the marks have been added up correctly, and that the mark on the script has been transferred correctly to the mark-sheet, which will be machine-read to transfer the marks to the computer.

This checking is vital, since there is plenty of scope for error. Quite apart from mathematical errors (and I wonder how many of us could add up the marks on, say, 300 scripts without making a single error) and the possibility of turning over two pages of a script at once and so missing a page, there are two tempting traps leading to clerical error. The first is that on the top of the script there is another number in addition to the mark awarded, namely the candidate number. It is all too easy to enter this on the mark-sheet rather than the mark, especially if it is very similar to the mark actually scored. Naturally if candidate number 1 or candidate number 1234 has scored 50 marks the examiner will not slip into error. But if candidate number 60 has done so, the error is easy to make. Second, to enter the mark onto a machine-read mark-sheet the examiner is normally required to shade in two lozenges on the sheet, one for the tens and another for the units. It is quite easy to get these the wrong way round, so that a candidate who scored, say, 71 could end up, disastrously, with only 17 (or of course vice versa).

The second stage of the clerical check is carried out in the offices of the Board (as in fact the first would have been if for any reason the examiner had not been able to employ a checker). This second stage consists of verifying that the mark held on the computer is the same as that recorded on the script. This might not be so if the mark-sheet has been stained or damaged in some way, or the entries were made on it with a writing implement which the reading machine cannot detect. These readers are designed to reject unreadable sheets, so that the operator can enter such marks manually, but inevitably there will be cases where the machine believes that it has read the sheet correctly and so does not throw it out for human action. The Boards employ large numbers of temporary clerks to undertake this work, and the number of errors which they discover is certainly sufficient to justify the time and money spent.

This two-stage check should ensure that if the marking has been correct the grade awarded will be correct. In fact, of course, it still cannot be perfect. Checkers can be careless in what is a tedious task – and some can be irresponsible. I recall one case of a checker who 'corrected' several of the original marks, unfortunately changing what had been right to what was wrong! Happily this was discovered during the grade review (and neither the examiner nor his checker employed again). Similarly, temporary clerks checking thousands of scripts over a week or two can become bored and read what they expect to find. Despite the many errors which are detected and corrected, every year odd ones are found to have slipped through the net and are only discovered during a result enquiry from the Centre after the results have been issued.

THE GRADE REVIEW

The second safety net is the grade review. This is an exercise carried out by a small team of senior examiners after every other process has taken place, and it consists of reviewing the scripts of all candidates 'at risk'. The standardization of the examining team should have ironed out any significant errors of marking. During the marking process every Assistant Examiner will have sent samples of scripts to the Principal Examiner or Team Leader. This will have enabled the Principal Examiner to guide the examiner, all being well, to a consistently correct standard, or at the worst will have enabled the Principal Examiner to recommend that the examiner's marking be adjusted by scaling. This can be a consistent adjustment, for instance the addition of a fixed number of marks to all scripts marked by a severe examiner or subtraction from those marked by a lenient examiner, or could be graduated if the examiner has been lenient to the best but harsh to the worst (or vice versa) as some are. In such a case, for example, one might have a scale of –3 for marks over 70, –2 for marks in the range of 69–60, –1 for marks of 59–50, no change for marks of 49–40, +1 for marks of 39–30 and +2 for marks below 30. In cases of erratic examining, of course, such scaling is impossible (and even at its best one has to admit that scaling is a blunt instrument; no examiner is perfectly consistent in deviation from the correct line). In this case the Principal Examiner might have no alternative but to recommend that all the scripts marked by that examiner should be re-marked (and the examiner not re-employed!).

This category of candidates, those marked by an unsatisfactory examiner, is the first category of those 'at risk'. The Code of Practice requires their scripts to be re-marked if their aggregate marks are 'one per cent or less below the C/D grade boundary (GCSE), or B/C or E/N boundaries (GCE)'. Clearly this is much too limited a requirement, and I believe that every Board does more than this minimum. In fact 'one per cent or less' is the sort of error that any examiner, even the best, might occasionally make, let alone one who has been identified as unsatisfactory, and such errors will not be confined to the boundaries which the Code identifies. Nor is it reasonable to assume that only those identified boundaries are important; only the candidate knows in his particular personal circumstances which boundaries matter. With university places often hanging on precise offers at A Level in particular, it is wrong to value some boundaries more highly than others.

If standardization has been done properly each Principal Examiner will be able to identify for the grade review team the features of the work of each examiner which make that examiner unsatisfactory. If the marking is wildly erratic then probably every script will have to be re-marked, but in some cases the unsatisfactory marking may be confined to particular questions or sections of the paper. For instance, in a paper involving literature, whether in English or another language, there is usually a choice of prescribed texts. The examiner may be very familiar with some, but much less so with others, and the reliability of marking on any particular script will depend upon the texts on which that candidate has chosen to answer. Accordingly the grade review team will re-mark scripts in line with the briefing which the Principal Examiner is able to give. I should then expect them to re-mark scripts at each grade boundary and to cover a range of marks identified by the Principal Examiner wide enough to allow for whatever variation has been identified in the original marking.

Two other criteria identified by the Code of Practice as pointing to a candidate 'at risk' are 'marked discrepancies between estimated grades and provisional grades' and 'markedly atypical profiles'. Boards do not use these criteria automatically as a trigger to re-mark scripts in all circumstances, although if coupled with a second factor, in particular if the candidate is within striking distance of a grade boundary, they will probably trigger at the very least a quick look at the aberrant script. For instance, if the Centre has fore-cast grade A for a candidate who is in fact awarded grade C (a discrepancy of two grades normally being regarded as the minimum to attract consideration) this may indicate an error in the marking. On the other hand, many candidates do in fact fall two grades short of expectation, and bearing in mind that the forecast may well have erred on the optimistic side, the candidate need not have fallen far below form for this apparent discrepancy to have appeared.

Similarly, a candidate with an 'atypical profile', for instance four components graded A, B, A, E, might well have been the victim of aberrant marking on the fourth component. However, many can-didates do in fact have a weak spot in their grasp of the subject, and if the four components test different skills or different areas of con-tent, as they probably do since there would be no point in having four components if that were not so, one component out of line with the others may not be surprising.

In dealing with both these criteria I should expect a further cler-ical check to be carried out if the grade review is to be done properly. Discrepancies of this sort, several grades between forecast and actu-ality or between different components, are not resolved by minor adjustments of a mark or two. If they are genuine evidence of error they are pointing at major error, only explicable by failure to add up or record the marks correctly or the complete missing of a page or two. It is only worth re-marking the scripts in their entirety if the mark is also very close to a grade boundary, in which case very small adjustments, which are quite typical of a re-mark, would modify, but not entirely remove, the anomaly.

Normal practice at a grade review, therefore, is to re-mark the scripts of aberrant examiners, following criteria identified by the Chief and Principal Examiners, and only to carry out a full re-mark otherwise if more than one factor applies, usually one of the crite-ria identified above coupled with close proximity to a grade boundary. Boards also commonly limit the re-mark to identified boundaries, particularly for GCSE where the C/D boundary (in terms which are now 'politically incorrect', the pass/fail boundary) is seen as crucial. At A Level more boundaries may be covered, particularly in small-entry subjects. When the Principal Examiners for Russian, for instance, meet, they will probably have dealt with all the scripts covered by the compulsory criteria by lunchtime; they might as well remain an hour or two and widen the criteria. On the other hand, for a subject such as English it is hard enough to meet the compulsory criteria over several days, let alone to widen the criteria. Nor could the problem be solved by employing a larger grade review team, since the key to the activity is that the most senior and experienced examiners are reviewing scripts marked by their assistants. It would negate that principle if assistants were added to the team.

It may be noted that scripts just above a grade boundary are not re-marked unless they are covered by the complete re-marking of the work of an aberrant examiner. A candidate one mark above the grade boundary, or indeed on the boundary itself, and having scored grade A when forecast C, will not be subject to a re-mark. Candidates who benefit from errors of marking are not considered to be 'at risk', nor are they by a normal understanding of that phrase. Similarly at later stages of the process, enquiry and appeal, subject grades are not reduced even if they are then found to be incorrect (although an exception is made for module marks when the module is being banked and the mark has not yet been used for aggregation at syllabus level). This is understandable after publication; but at grade review, before the results have been published, there would be a good case to check such scripts, and it is only the limited resources, human and time, which prevent its being done.

It may well appear that the criteria for grade review will not lead to the detection of every error. Only the complete re-marking of the work of all the candidates could achieve that, and a full re-mark is simply not practicable. In reality, however, the mark of any script is not likely to be adjusted by more than a mark or two, and therefore it is not important if scripts well below the boundaries are not re-marked, since any change to script marks would be highly unlikely to change the grade. What is important, to my mind, is that scripts adjacent to every boundary, not just those identified as 'key', should be re-marked. When this is not done, the Boards are not providing proper quality control.

THE GRADE REVIEW IN MODULAR SYLLABUSES

The development of modular syllabuses has added an extra problem. In the traditional linear format one could identify those candidates a mark or two below a grade boundary at subject level, and then re-mark all the components, since an additional mark on any one of the components might affect the subject grade. But when a module is taken at an early session there is no means of knowing how close the candidate will eventually be to a grade boundary at subject level. From this point of view the grade boundary at module level is irrelevant; the candidate one mark below the module boundary may achieve the grade comfortably at subject level if later modules produce a better result. Similarly, a candidate achieving a good module grade might fall a single mark short at subject level because of weaker performances later. There is clearly a case for withholding the results of early modules and conducting a full grade review at the end of the course, but this would not do since some candidates need the early results as they plan the next stage: for instance, they need to know whether they ought to re-sit the module. Moreover, they need to know the exact mark which they are carrying forward, not an approximate mark subject to later review. Nor could the Boards conveniently store such an abundance of scripts, which may have a shelf-life of up to four years if the candidate so desires.

For these reasons the only criterion applicable at module level is that of the script having been marked by an aberrant examiner. This puts the greatest possible weight upon the primary marking being correct, since there will be no grade review of all of a candidate's work at the end of a modular course: each module will be treated in isolation. Moreover, when the subject grade is published an enquiry or appeal concerning modules taken other than in the final session will not be possible since the scripts will no longer exist. By not challenging the results of early modules at the time when they were issued the candidate has forgone the opportunity to do so later.

This procedure is, not surprisingly, controversial. The Code of Practice does not at present require the Boards to consider any criteria in reviewing module marks other than that of an aberrant examiner. It is at least plausible to argue that what one cannot do for one candidate one should not do for others, so that, if some candidates spread the modules over many sessions while others perhaps take them all at one sitting, it would be wrong to apply a wider range of criteria to the latter – which would be possible – since they cannot be applied to the former. On the other hand, there are those who argue that the priority must lie in getting the results right, and that to ignore pointers to possible error in the case of some candidates merely because they cannot be applied in others amounts to a deliberate act of injustice. It is certainly the case that in some subjects, primarily in the field of arts and humanities, many candidates, perhaps even a substantial majority, take all the modules at the final session. In effect they are linear candidates; all the criteria can be applied and all the work is available.

It should be noted that the Code of Practice lays down a minimum requirement. There is no reason why a Board should not exceed that; and some, I am sure, do, at least in some subjects. There is, however, a danger that Boards will keep to the minimum, partly for reasons of cost and time, and partly because their computer software is written to treat modular syllabuses as a set of separate modules and does not have the facility written in conveniently to identify criteria which arise from a view across the full suite.

RESULT ENQUIRIES: THE PRACTICALITIES

However the Boards conduct the grade review, in terms of keeping to the minimum requirement or expanding it, such a review will always have taken place before the results are published. The Boards themselves have no wish for any published grade subsequently to be found to be wrong. In such a case they can only lose: financially in putting it right; in future sessions by an increase in post-publication challenges to the results if public confidence is undermined; in the long term by Centres who have suffered possibly moving their entries to another Board. If errors remain after publication it is not because the Boards have wilfully failed in their duty, but because it has not been possible in the time available to carry out even more checks.

A candidate wishing to challenge a published result may do so by initiating a result enquiry. Here, to get the terminology right, we should note that this is not an appeal. The term 'appeal' is reserved for a later stage of the process, when an enquiry has left the candidate still wishing to challenge the result. An enquiry may ask for a clerical check, a re-mark of the scripts, a re-mark accompanied by a report, and/or re-moderation of coursework.

The enormous proliferation in recent years of enquiries upon results is, in my opinion, the greatest threat to the smooth running of the examination process. It has become a burden which is beginning to drive away some of the very best examiners, without whom examinations will not happen. When one accepts the post of Chief or Principal Examiner one knows that there will be three major tasks: setting question papers, marking and standardizing the marking of scripts, grading and reviewing the results. These can be fitted into one's working and personal life without too much difficulty: question papers can be set in the school holidays or at weekends; marking will be in the latter part of the term or perhaps early in the school holidays; grading and grade review will usually be in the holidays. But result enquiries are unpredictable, very urgent, and usually fall at the beginning of the autumn term, when teachers are deeply involved in moving into a new academic year, with new pupils and new challenges of their own to face. I know of examiners who have declined to carry out result enquiries, and if the Board insists that this is such an integral part of the role that they cannot continue to be employed if they are not prepared to do it, they have chosen to stand down. The examining process cannot afford to lose its best examiners, and all the candidates are likely to suffer if this happens. I am sure that greater control needs to be brought to the enquiry process.

It is perhaps not surprising that the demand for enquiries has increased as it has. The introduction of league tables, recording the performances of schools and setting them against one another, has made it much more pressing for schools to maximize their results. Headteachers are more and more likely to put pressure upon the subject teachers, whose best defence may seem to be to argue that the Board must have got the results wrong, and therefore to challenge them, perhaps more in hope than expectation. Small departments in some schools may find themselves closed down if their results are poor. Why continue to teach Russian or Geology if all your candidates do badly? Parents too can be pressing, and it may be easier to offer to challenge the result than to tell fond parents that their son or daughter is not as bright as they thought. (I recall a candidate forecast to obtain grade C, actually awarded grade B, and submitting an enquiry. The headteacher, in a prestigious independent school at which the parents were paying substantial fees, admitted to the Board that the parents had been led to believe that grade A had been forecast for their son! He was submitting an enquiry rather than confess the truth to the parents.)

The major problem in providing a quick enquiry procedure lies in the service whereby a report is provided by the examiner who re-marks the script. It is of course understandable that the Centre may wish to discover what weaknesses there had been in the candidate's work and so to improve future teaching, or to guide the candidate in cases where a re-sit is necessary. More cynically, they may wish to satisfy themselves that the examiner has actually carried out the re-mark! I can understand that a Centre which simply asked for a re-mark and received the response that there had been no change to the marks might wonder whether the examiner had troubled to read the script again. (Indeed I recall an appeal of a few years ago in A-Level French in which the appellant's main ground of appeal was that on re-mark no change had been made to the marks. He argued that over five components, some involving essays, some changes of marks, however trivial, in one direction or the other, would have been certain if the re-mark had been carried out properly!)

The disadvantage is that the production of a report takes time. Even a lengthy script may be re-marked by an experienced examiner in twenty minutes, but a report, produced clearly and legibly in a form which can be transmitted to the Centre without re-typing, as the Boards require, could take a further hour. If the morning's post brings half a dozen scripts for re-mark, three requiring a report and three not, the examiner, at the end of a normal day's work and probably with work to mark and lessons to prepare for the following day, is likely to tackle only those scripts requiring a simple re-mark, and to postpone the others until the next day, or the weekend; but the next morning may bring as many scripts again.

To the candidate, speed of response is important; in the case of A Level a university place may be at stake. I am sure that somehow the process must be streamlined and I go back to my early experience to suggest how this could be done. When I was first a Board officer my Board was just introducing its enquiry system (after over a century in which there had been no provision of any kind for candidates to challenge the results!). As part of the process the Secretary at that time retained the right to reject enquiries. There were two grounds on which this might be done: the first was because the scripts had already been re-marked during the grade review; the second was that the candidate had achieved or bettered the grade forecast by the Centre. If enquiries could be rejected on these two grounds – and the former seems particularly strong – or moved to the back of the queue, on the basis that it is highly unlikely that a re-mark will make any difference, those with a real prospect of success could be dealt with more quickly.

The current procedures, though logical in themselves, inevitably create delay. When I was first involved in this process all a candidate's component scripts were sent to the same senior examiner. The Board would have identified examiners who were available – in late August many are still justifiably on holiday – and would know which ones were normally able to respond quickly. The disadvantage was that no single examiner had done primary marking on all the components, but a single examiner, however senior, was now being asked to be the final arbiter on work including material of which he had no direct experience. This is no longer permitted; each component must be re-marked by an examiner who has done primary marking of that component. Whenever possible this will be the Principal Examiner, but in some cases a script will be referred which he himself had marked in the first place. Since it seems highly unlikely that he would admit to previous error and correct his own work (although I have known cases where this has happened) such a script will be referred to someone else in the examining team. I am actually not convinced that such an examiner will be prepared to correct the work of his superior, and I can imagine the outcome of an unsuccessful enquiry being challenged on that ground, but such is the requirement at the moment.

The need to send each component to a separate examiner takes time. At its lowest, a clerk in the Board's offices must address and despatch perhaps four envelopes rather than one. The responses also will come back in different envelopes, probably on different days, and will have to be amalgamated before a decision is reached. And of course the Centre will not receive a response until the slowest of the examiners has replied. However rapid and conscientious the great majority may be, if a quarter of the examiners are slow, probably for very understandable reasons, virtually all the replies to Centres will be slow.

Nor is the outcome of an enquiry the end of the matter if it gives rise to a change of grade. The Code of Practice requires the Boards to 'take whatever steps they consider appropriate to protect the interests of all candidates who may have been similarly affected', in any case where the outcome of an enquiry 'is such as to bring into question the accuracy of results for other candidates in the same examination'. Now if an enquiry changes a mark it is hard to see why a re-mark of every other candidate marked by that examiner could not potentially do the same. True, some will have been checked as the examiners' standardization sample; some may have been checked at grade review; to some, if they already have grade A, it will be irrelevant. But many will be left where the error could exist, however unlikely. An examiner may have made a crashing error once; he may never make it again, but all the scripts will have to be checked to make sure. If I were a senior examiner re-marking a script and I found an error, I wonder how I should react to the thought that by reporting it I could land myself with the burden of checking perhaps two or three hundred more? I actually know of examiners who have honourably shouldered that burden; I do not know of any examiner who has reported dishonestly to avoid it. But the whole point is that such examiners would not be known.

RESULT ENQUIRIES: THEIR RELIABILITY

There is a further artificiality about result enquiries, and this turns on the state of mind in which the examiner carries them out. The very fact of an enquiry gives a suggestion that there may be something wrong with the original marking. Clearly someone thinks so, or the enquiry would not have been lodged. I have had examiners say to me, 'I can give this an extra two or three marks if you like'. But what I like is not the point. Does the script actually merit two or three more marks? And here one has to replicate somehow the mind-set of the original marking. When the original mark was given, the examiner was marking the script as one of perhaps two or three hundred. Matters of fact will not have changed, of course, but matters of judgement may have blurred. At the first time of asking the examiner marking an essay out of 25 may have hovered between 15 and 16, and finally settled on 15. If at re-mark the examiner settles on 16 is this a genuine change, or a change because the work is being looked at in isolation, after several weeks' gap in which the examiner has done no work of this kind? My belief is that, while errors of demonstrable fact must always be corrected, changes to judgemental decisions should only be made, if at all, when the examiner is certain beyond all possible doubt that the change is justified. If the change is merely being made because of the changed context in which the work is being considered, it could mean that the candidate is no longer being marked to the standards applied at the time of the original marking, the standard applied to all the other candidates, the standard to which the grading decisions were geared.

The other side of this coin is that some examiners may be provoked to harshness by an enquiry. 'How dare they challenge our marking?' may be in the minds of some examiners, and a tendency, even if not acknowledged, to give nothing away. I have certainly known examiners who more often than not raised a mark on enquiry and others who almost never did so, or even wanted to reduce the mark. I find it hard to believe that by pure chance the former had more than their fair share of under-marked scripts and the latter the reverse. Boards have of course worked very hard to train examiners to a proper way of thinking, and not to use examiners for this key work if their reliability is open to question. Nevertheless, my reservations about the whole process remain, both in terms of its practicality and its efficiency.

APPEALS

If the Centre or the candidate remain dissatisfied with the result of the enquiry they may appeal. This can be a two-stage process, in the first instance to the Board's own Appeals Committee and, if they remain dissatisfied even then, to the Independent Appeals Authority for School Examinations (IAASE). However, it must be understood that at this stage the issue moves from that of the academic quality of the candidate's scripts to that of the procedures followed. The Appeals Committees, both that of the Board and IAASE, are small bodies – probably five or six people in the former case and normally three in the latter. Although each member will have expertise in a particular subject, it is quite possible that none of them will have expertise in the subject involved in the appeal. The ultimate arbiter of the standard of the script itself is the Chief Examiner for that syllabus, supported by the Principal Examiners. It was they who set the standards and took a leading role in the grading decisions. If an outside body were to decide that they were wrong in the assessment of a candidate, the only conclusion possible would be that they were likely to be wrong in their assessment of all the candidates. That examination would be invalidated. Even if a member or members of the Appeals Committee happened to be expert in the subject in question, they would not have done any marking of that particular set of question papers; they would not have seen the standard being produced by all the candidates, in which context the work of the appellant is to be judged. On what basis could they judge that the original decisions were wrong?

The only possible subject-specific resource which they have, and one which has been used occasionally, is to require a Chief Examiner from another Board to give advice, or to supervise a re-mark of disputed work. Even so, such a person has not been intimately involved with the work and is inevitably bringing a less than perfect view of that particular syllabus and set of question papers to bear. If it is no longer permitted within one Board for the Principal Examiner for one component to conduct the re-mark of another, as is the case for result enquiries, how much less appropriate is it for an examiner from another Board to do so?

For this reason Appeals Committees deal only with procedures. If the appellant can show that the Board has not met the requirements of the Code of Practice and has not followed its own internal procedures, the appeal will succeed; but this does not mean that the grade will be raised. The Committee will rule that the candidate's work should be re-assessed (and possibly the work of some or all of the other candidates too) in accordance with proper procedures. Almost always when this is the verdict the re-assessment is carried out and leads to precisely the same grade being awarded. I suspect (although it is a pure guess) that a majority of successful appellants have ultimately gained no benefit whatever from their success.

This is not surprising. How can an appellant know whether or not the Board has followed procedures correctly? To the Centre a result has been issued which they find unbelievably bad. An enquiry has led to no change, and the report – assuming they applied for one – does not convince them that the candidate performed so badly as to justify the low grade awarded. To appeal they must allege some procedural failing, and what it might have been they have to guess.

On that basis many appeals could be rejected unheard, since Centres find it hard to produce a case to answer, but Boards are reluctant to reject appeals out of hand because of the highly adverse impression it would create – and the IAASE takes a similar view. Public confidence in the examinations demands proper investigation.

Those cases are in my view most difficult in which a whole group of candidates from a Centre has performed seriously below reasonable expectation. In every examination – probably in every school – there will be individual candidates whose performance is far out of line. These examinations are stressful and candidates do collapse under pressure. If in a batch of otherwise normal performances one candidate is given a below-par result it is almost certainly correct. Since the script will have been marked by the same examiner as all the others in the batch it would be extraordinary if the examiner marked incorrectly in the case of one candidate and one only, and the grade review is also likely to have checked such an anomalous performance. When an enquiry has confirmed the result, an appeal must be pointless. Certainly the procedures applied to the candidate can only be the same as those applied to the others, and therefore there will be no ground for a procedural appeal.

However, we have all met cases every year where the results of a complete set of candidates in one subject in one Centre are beyond dispute out of line. The Centre will point out, and prove with full detail, that in that subject for the last X years its results have been in line with its results in all other subjects. It will show that the candidates concerned have all performed fully as expected in their other subjects. It will assert, no doubt truthfully, that the teachers are the same as in the previous years and that their timetable allowance for the subject has not changed. It seems to follow that something must have gone wrong on the examining side.

The Boards always take these cases seriously because the evidence is convincing, and the possibility exists that that batch was marked badly and the error has gone unnoticed. Even a good examiner whose standardization samples have been entirely in line might, for instance, have fallen behind schedule at some point and marked right through the night to catch up. If those scripts were badly marked for that reason and none of them happened to be in the standardization sample, this unsatisfactory marking could escape undetected. However, if a result enquiry confirms the original marks as correct, what then? The Centre will appeal; everyone will 'know' that the results are wrong, yet every check shows that the marks and grades are a correct representation of what those candidates wrote in the examination room.

This is where I believe that the exact context of the examination is crucial, and why I think that examination results should not be given the definitive credence which they widely hold. When an appeal is launched, three, four, or even more months after the candidates actually sat in the examination room, it is virtually impossible to reconstruct the exact circumstances of the examination. But it is there where I feel the answer must lie. Was it a particularly hot, or cold, or stormy day? In the case of an afternoon paper, had those candidates had a long and difficult examination in another subject in the morning? In the case of a morning paper had they a long and difficult paper to come in another subject in the afternoon, to which they might have given most of their revision attention the previous evening? Were there distracting social activities taking place in the school at the time? At the end of the summer term it is not uncommon for schools to hold Speech Day, Sports Day, a school concert, a school dance, while examinations in the later stages of the timetable may still be taking place. If the candidates are involved in these things their minds could easily be divided. Just as those who own a car which repeatedly goes wrong speak of a 'Friday afternoon car', is there such a thing as a 'Friday afternoon examination performance'?

In my experience it is the failure to resolve this problem which is the greatest source of friction between Boards and Centres; it is this sort of dissatisfaction more than any other which persuades a Centre to switch its entries from one Board to another. But I am sure that both sides are in the right, and both have done their very best to resolve the problem in the best interests of the candidates.

One can only reiterate that examinations do not record what the grades ought to be, but what they actually were on the day.

SCRUTINIES

So far this chapter has discussed internal quality controls applied within the Board (with the exception of the role of the IAASE which is, of course, external). However, the Boards are not free from externally applied quality controls, the foremost of which lies in the Qualifications and Curriculum Authority (QCA). This body has already been mentioned with reference to its work in producing subject criteria, approving syllabuses and collaborating with the Boards in writing the Code of Practice. Its work of carrying out scrutinies was also mentioned briefly in Chapter 5, and we must look at this more fully now.

The QCA organizes scrutinies to a careful timetable to ensure that every Board will be subject to scrutiny each year in four or five subjects, and that every major subject will be scrutinized each year in at least one Board. After a few years very few syllabuses will have escaped attention. The scrutiny teams consist of very experienced senior examiners or former senior examiners from Boards other than the one being scrutinized. They know how procedures work and should be put into practice because they have done so themselves. They have their own established view of standards, as exemplified in question papers, mark-schemes and grading decisions, by virtue of having produced such papers and made such decisions in their own Boards. They may well in their turn have been subject to scrutiny, and if not they are likely to be so before long. Nor will they let off lightly those whom they scrutinize, since at the back of their minds will be an awareness of professional and commercial rivalry: although representing the QCA as scrutineers, they are also employed by Boards in direct rivalry with the one which they are scrutinizing.

At every stage of the examining process a scrutineer will be present. The only possible exception to this is the meeting at which the question papers are finalized, since it is normally held so far in advance of the examination, usually over a year ahead and sometimes nearer two, that at that stage the scrutiny team may well not have been appointed. However, of all stages of the process the question paper is the one which most openly speaks for itself later, without the absolute need to witness its evolution. Thus, with that exception, a scrutineer will be present at the standardization meeting of the examining team on each component, at the grading meeting, and will probably attend part, though not usually all, of the grade review. The Board is expected to make all relevant documentation available to the scrutineers, including procedural documents, archive scripts and relevant statistical data. It may have no secrets. When the grading is over and scripts can at last be spared out of the Board's hands, the scrutiny team will also be provided with whatever scripts they request, usually a range across key boundaries, so that they can mark them for themselves and satisfy themselves by their own trials that the marking has been done correctly and that they agree with the grading judgements.

The final stage is a meeting of the scrutiny team, normally for a day and a half or two days, in the offices of the Board. Having attended the previous stages individually, one observing one stage of the process and another another, this is their first real opportunity to compare notes and combine their findings. They also take this opportunity to seek clarification on doubtful points from the Board's staff; for instance, if they were unhappy with the marking or grading of any of the scripts which they have seen they may now ask for further scripts on the mark in question or marked by the examiner whose work troubles them. On the second afternoon at the Board they meet together with the senior examining team whose work they are scrutinizing. At this meeting all their findings will be discussed (as a matter of principle the final report will not include criticisms of which the Board has not been informed at this stage) and it gives a last opportunity for the Board to justify itself if it has an answer to the points raised. The discussion is carefully structured, following a briefing document provided by the QCA, which ensures that no aspect of the whole process can be overlooked.

The report eventually will be full and frank, and a wise Board will welcome it and act upon it. When I was myself a Board officer I occasionally found such a report very helpful in guiding examiners who thought that the rules did not apply to them or to their subject! My only dissatisfactions were when one year's report contradicted that of the year before in a related subject (e.g. French in one year and German the next, in which the syllabuses were identical), or when a scrutiny criticized the structure of a syllabus which the QCA had itself approved. Indeed I recall strong criticism of one detail of a syllabus which had been inserted originally against the Board's wishes but on the insistence of the QCA (or more accurately SCAA as it was then called). On the whole, however, scrutinies give an excellent guarantee to the public that the examinations are being properly run.

PROBES

The QCA also has a second weapon in its armoury, namely probes. A probe may be launched if subsequent to the publication of the results there seems to be reason to fear that the standards applied were incorrect. This may apply if the percentage of candidates obtaining top grades in a syllabus has changed dramatically from one year to the next and if the Board cannot provide a convincing explanation. Sometimes changes of entry patterns explain such a change. For instance, a few years ago in GCSE there was a sharp migration of candidates away from three separate sciences (Physics, Chemistry and Biology) to a single composite Science syllabus. But the very best continued to offer the separate sciences, while the weaker candidates took the more general subject, with the result that statistically the results in the separate subjects appeared to have improved dramatically. This was of course explicable without the need for a probe to investigate it.

The fact that a probe can only be launched after the event restricts its scope. Obviously no one can witness the stages of the process since they have already happened. But the QCA can arrange for suitable people, qualified as for a scrutiny, to be sent scripts at key boundaries and all relevant statistical data. It can then check whether the scripts have been marked and graded correctly. I have myself only experienced one probe, the findings of which were that the Board had been generous – but only slightly so. Nevertheless, the possibility of a probe represents a useful additional check in any case where anxiety is aroused.

OFSTED

The QCA is not the only official body keeping an eye on standards, since OFSTED also can become involved. From time to time OFSTED conducts inspections of a subject in a Board, although in my experience in a more limited way than the QCA. This involves an inspector attending the various stages of the process, as the QCA's scrutineers do, but without the final stages of scripts being marked by the inspector and a meeting with the Board. The primary question being asked is whether the Code of Practice is being followed. If so it is accepted that the examining team will arrive at the right decisions; if not the report is more likely to say that it is impossible to know whether the standards are right or wrong rather than to declare them wrong.

From all the above it can be seen that everything humanly possible is done to ensure that the results awarded are a correct representation of the candidate's performance in the examination room. More than that they cannot be.

Chapter 7

Candidates and Their Problems

The previous chapters have had a lot to say about procedures. One might think that we are dealing with an industrial process. In fact, of course, we are dealing with candidates for whom the result may be a turning-point in their lives. GCSE grades may well determine the choice of A-Level subjects; A-Level grades may secure, or not, a university place or a much-desired job. Unsatisfactory results may lead to inferior employment, or perhaps to the loss of a year of the candidate's life if a re-take year is found to be necessary.

Candidates taking an examination may in one sense seem to be caught up in a machine, but they are of course very human and subject to all the problems of a human being: they may be ill or late for the examination because of a traffic problem; they may have been taught the wrong material, or entered for the wrong option; and sometimes they cheat.

Illnesses of one sort and another, physical or psychological, are very common. Over six weeks in the summer many thousands of young people in the ordinary course of events will be ill, have accidents, or experience the death of a relative or friend. The Boards will make every effort to ensure that all candidates are given the 'right' results and it is desirable to explore this concept more fully.

TEMPORARY AND PERMANENT HANDICAPS

There are two kinds of disability: temporary and permanent. The former, much the commoner, are relatively easy to deal with because they have no lasting effect upon the candidate's ability. A candidate working with a broken arm might score grade B, and the Board may be satisfied, on inspection of the evidence, that without the handicap the candidate would have achieved grade A. Grade A will therefore be awarded, and this result will in no way mislead subsequent users, since when the arm is healed the candidate will again be able to produce grade A work. If the next stage of the candidate's educational or working life depends upon the grade A, it will not have been wrong to award it.

The situation is very different if the candidate suffers a permanent disability. If such a candidate produces grade B work it would be wrong to award grade A, even if one were satisfied that without the handicap the candidate would have achieved grade A. The fact is that the candidate will never be without the handicap and will therefore never be able to produce grade A work.

THE PERMANENTLY HANDICAPPED

The procedure for candidates with a permanent handicap is to make whatever arrangements are possible for them to perform to the best of their ability, but not to adjust the result thereafter. Thus, a visually handicapped candidate may be given an enlarged question paper with extra bold type, or a braille paper if he is fully blind; a candidate physically incapable of writing will be allowed an amanuensis; a candidate physically unable to sit throughout the full length of the examination will be allowed rest breaks. The deaf and dumb, who by virtue of their handicap often have a very limited reading vocabulary, will be provided with a modified question paper using the simplest possible language. Other candidates, such as the dyslexic, will be allowed additional time to write their answers. If such arrangements mean that some of the assessment objectives cannot be met, the certificate will be endorsed to indicate the fact. For instance, a deaf and dumb candidate taking French would not be able to attempt the listening and speaking tests, and so would be graded on the skills of reading and writing and given an endorsed grade.

On the whole, candidates with permanent disabilities are content with the way they are treated in examinations. In the ordinary course of their education they will have become accustomed to special arrangements being made for them to do their work, and will expect to be examined by the same methods. The worse the handicap, the less problem the Boards usually have. The blind candidate expects to be treated as such, and certainly knows that her blindness cannot be concealed from a future employer, so that there is no point in attempting to gain inflated results in the examination. The two disabilities which in my experience give the greatest problems are hay fever and dyslexia.

Hay fever is in one sense a permanent disability but cannot be treated as such. A medical note stating that 'this candidate is liable to be adversely affected by hay fever during the period of the examination' – and I have seen such notes – is worthless. It is doubtless a true statement, but however much the candidate may have suffered in some sessions, there may have been others in which the pollen count was minimal, the rain fell and the wind blew. What is needed is a statement session by session, indicating whether the candidate was actually suffering from an attack of hay fever at that time, and how severely. It will then be treated as a temporary handicap.

Dyslexia is the most contentious affliction of all. It is certainly permanent and is normally dealt with by the allowance of extra time, up to 25 per cent extra onto the time of the examination. Whether this is appropriate I am not sure. I certainly recall one candidate who objected on the ground that the longer he wrote the worse his work became! My response that perhaps he would prefer to be given a reduced time was regarded (rightly!) as facetious, and he ended by being allowed the extra time, since no one has thought of a more convincing alternative, although

I never discovered whether he actually took advantage of it.

Dyslexic candidates can be exempt from the requirements of spelling, punctuation and grammar (SPAG) for GCSE, but in this case the certificate will be endorsed. Since SPAG carries only 5% of the marks, candidates in general choose not to seek exemption. Only if the candidate falls short of a grade boundary by 5% or less would exemption from the requirement be of any benefit. In other cases granting exemption would not affect the grade issued, while the endorsement would highlight to any future user of the certificate a handicap which the candidate may wish to play down. Even when exemption is claimed and endorsement accepted, one may wonder whether the advantage of one grade higher with endorsement was greater than that of the lower grade without endorsement.

CANDIDATES WHO MISS PART OF THE COURSE

Related to permanent handicaps, although not strictly permanent, are cases where a candidate has missed part of the course, usually because of a protracted period of illness, but sometimes because of the absence of a teacher whom the school has been unable to replace. In normal circumstances the Board will make no allowance for this, and such an attitude is understandable. If the candidate has not studied part of the course it is impossible to guess how well he would have fared if he had done it. Performance on other components is some sort of guide but cannot be conclusive. Candidates do not perform evenly on all parts of the course and on all components (if they did, examinations consisting of one component would be quite sufficient). Sometimes, of course, the missing item may be so closely akin to one which has been covered that it may be possible to make an allowance. For instance, if the course included two plays of Shakespeare but only one had been studied, it might be fair to assume that the marks on the play missed would have been little different from the one read. However, it is rare for the gap to be as closely related as this to material studied.

Of course it seems hard that the candidate can receive no compensation for such a gap, and so must attempt the examination unprepared and accept the mark scored without adjustment. Yet in terms of the next step this is realistic. The gap in knowledge or skill exists, and it is unhelpful to pretend that it does not. A candidate moving on to the next stage without filling the gap, whether from GCSE to A Level or from A Level to university, could be at a serious disadvantage at that stage. It is often better for the candidate to delay a year and repeat the course, thus being able to go ahead with a proper foundation.

CANDIDATES ABSENT FOR PART OF THE EXAMINATION

The case of a candidate who has completed the course but is then obliged through no fault of her own to miss part of the examination is rather different. If an allowance can be made which seems right in line with the available evidence, the grade awarded would not be misleading; the candidate would be ready to move on to the next stage. Of course there must be sufficient evidence; a result cannot be awarded if the candidate misses the whole examination. If possible one would wish 50% of the assessment to have been completed, but 35% is commonly accepted as adequate, and this is realistic in view of the structure of many syllabuses. I know of one (and doubtless there are many similar) where the components divide 55%/45%. It is obviously unjust if a candidate who takes the first part and then falls ill for the second may have a result, while the candidate who is ill for the first paper but recovers in time for the second may not. This is why a smaller minimum is now allowed.

For a candidate in this position the evidence, in addition to any examination work completed, will be the forecast grade provided by the Centre and an indication of where the Centre expects the candidate to fall in their order of merit, by identifying two candidates whom they expect to come immediately above and two whom they expect to come immediately below the absent candidate. If their forecasting in the case of candidates whose work is completed is roughly correct (it is almost never perfect), and if the four identified candidates perform as expected relative to one another, there is little difficulty in awarding the absent candidate a grade which one can feel confident is right. Of course, when the Centre's forecasts turn out to be wrong and the comparable candidates perform erratically, with perhaps the expected better ones doing worse and vice versa, the grade becomes very difficult to award. However, candidates in this position can be sure that the Board will have done its best and that the decision will be a rational one.

If a candidate wakes on the morning of the examination feeling seriously ill, is it better to struggle in and attempt the examination, or to stay in bed and trust to the part-absence procedure? Obviously this will depend upon how ill the candidate feels, but my own belief is that it is usually better to be absent. The procedure for compensating candidates who sit an examination while unwell (to be described below) seems to me to be markedly less generous than that for compensating part-absent candidates. I have certainly met cases of candidates who struggled in and fell a grade or two short of what they would have scored if they had stayed in bed.

Of course in the case of absent candidates the Board must be satisfied that the absence is legitimate. One could not allow the possibility of a candidate finding it profitable to be absent from his weakest component on the basis that he would then be given a mark for it commensurate with his best. Unequivocal medical evidence or other relevant evidence justifying the absence is essential. If no evidence is provided and no application for part-absence consideration is submitted, the candidate will be given no grade for the subject, whatever marks have been scored on the other components. Candidates are not permitted to treat the examination so lightly, nor can they opt for a mark of zero on a component without turning up (although a candidate who attends, writes his name on the top of the script, and otherwise hands in a blank sheet, will be given zero for that component and graded for the subject). I recall a case of a candidate who missed a component at A Level but had sufficient marks on the others already to reach grade C. Since no application for part-absence treatment had been received from the Centre we were afraid that it had gone astray, and so we telephoned the Centre to check. But no; the candidate had simply not turned up and had made no attempt to explain the absence. Although a mark of zero would have left him with grade C, no result was in fact awarded.

Sometimes it is difficult to determine whether or not an absence is legitimate. When the absence is for medical reasons there is not normally a problem, provided that the absence is supported by a doctor's note. However, there is a range of other personal and family grounds which may be debatable. Is attendance at a relative's wedding or funeral an adequate ground? Probably yes, if the relationship is close enough. However, I recall a case of a candidate who was herself being married and for whom this pretext for absence was not regarded as acceptable. Since she was presumably in control of her wedding date she could have chosen a different one. On the other hand, a candidate who gave birth on the day of the examination was allowed part-absence consideration. However much her own actions may have brought about the situation, she was not ultimately in control of the date!

What about a family holiday? This is almost certainly not acceptable as a ground for absence, since even if the date of the holiday is in some way dictated, for instance by the parents' employment, one could forgo a holiday when a key examination is at stake. What about a sporting commitment? This will probably only be allowable if the event is important enough. A candidate selected to represent the country at international level will almost certainly be given the full concession. At county level it is not very likely, while a school fixture will not earn exemption from an examination. The old days when candidates were given exemption if they were rowing for their schools at Henley or shooting at Bisley (and the examination timetables were sometimes worked out to fit round those events) are long gone!

LOST COURSEWORK

Another form of absence, although not absent in the strict sense, occurs if coursework is lost. Often this is not the fault of the candidate; it may have been lost by the teacher (bearing in mind that such work done in the early part of the course may have had to be stored for several months). If the work has been marked there is no problem; the Board can accept the marks and, since moderation in the normal sense will be impossible, it will have to make a decision whether to accept them as they stand (the usual outcome) or to adjust them in the light of the Centre's record of accuracy in the marking of its coursework and in the light of other relevant evidence such as forecast grades and performance in the actual examination. If the work has not been marked the same procedure will be applied as for absence from any other part of the examination. The same obviously has to apply also in those rare cases of examination scripts being lost in the post. From time to time a packet is posted off by a Centre, never to be seen again. It is of course more difficult to make part-absent decisions when all the scripts from a Centre in one of the components are lost. In such a case one cannot make judgements about one candidate in relation to the performance of the others. But although there is less evidence available, the Board will still ensure that a result is awarded to each candidate, and that that result can be justified rationally.

TIMETABLE DEVIATIONS

When a candidate's absence is known in advance there may be a good alternative, namely to allow the candidate to take the examination early, or late, provided that satisfactory arrangements can be made for the security of the question paper. I recall the cricketer David Bairstow, who subsequently kept wicket for England, making his debut for Yorkshire at the age of 17, having taken an A Level at 7.30 a.m. in time to complete it and take the field at Headingly by 11 a.m. Security is the key. When a candidate has taken an examination early, that candidate must be kept under close supervision until all the other candidates are safely in the examination room, not just in the Centre concerned but also in all other Centres throughout the country. Since all Centres have flexibility in starting the examination of up to half an hour after the official starting time, and since a candidate arriving late may be allowed to sit the examination, a candidate who has taken the examination early must be closely supervised until the examination has been completed in all Centres. With the technology available today, including mobile telephones, fax and e-mail, a candidate could very easily pass on vital information to a friend, given only a brief chance.

Similarly, if a candidate is to be allowed to take an examination late, she must be supervised from the first moment at which anyone who has taken the examination could have left the examination room until she herself is safely taking the examination. Sometimes that can even involve overnight supervision. The commonest reason is not in fact personal difficulties on the part of the candidate, but in many hundreds, and probably thousands, of cases every year it is caused by clashes in the timetable. The Boards make every effort to prevent this, and always agree upon the timetabling of major subjects so that a clash will not be possible; when one Board sets English so do all the others. But time constraints and the very large number of subjects now on offer make it inevitable that several minority subjects will fall into the same slot. There may even be clashes with a major subject; if one Board's syllabus has a component more than the others, that component will not be able to be set in a 'protected' slot. When several subjects have to be set in the same slot the Boards make every effort to pair together those which one candidate is not likely to take. In fact, however, no such pairing exists; one can merely keep the clashes to a minimum. When I was responsible for the timetable I recall pairing together German and Russian, in the expectation that no candidate would do both, only to find that in one Centre a group of candidates offered precisely that pairing.

If it proves necessary to allow some candidates to rearrange their timetables, the Board always prefers candidates to take the paper concerned after the official time rather than in advance. If malpractice were to take place when a paper had been sat early the whole candidature would be under suspicion, since the candidate who had seen the paper might have found some means of informing any other anywhere; if it is taken late the only candidate who could benefit from malpractice would be the late taker, and the Centre and Board know where to focus their attention and be on the alert.

Often I feel that such timetable changes, although inevitable (they would not be permitted if they were not), add stress to the candidates involved. If a candidate has to take lunch in the company of a teacher, isolated from his friends, must take any exercise or relaxation under the eye of a teacher, and must even go to the toilet with a teacher on guard, it cannot be the best preparation for an examination. How much worse if this situation pertains overnight. Candidates are sometimes put up overnight at the home of a teacher, and this cannot be easy for them. In a boarding school they may sleep in the sanatorium, but again will have to spend a long and lonely evening. For obvious reasons supervision at home by parents is not normally acceptable. (N.B. 'Normally' is perhaps the most valuable word in examination regulations. It indicates that the Board would not expect the principle to be breached, and cannot think of circumstances which might justify a breach, but leaves 'normally' written in to allow scope if something unforeseen arises.)

TEMPORARY HANDICAPS

Every year there are candidates suffering from a temporary handicap. Most of these will be physical, but there are also many cases of psychological difficulty and trauma, some very extreme. What of the candidate whose mother is suffering from terminal cancer and may die at any moment, and whose father is then killed in a road accident the day before the examination (an actual case which I recall)? What of the candidate idly watching from the bedroom window as a neighbour climbs a tree in his garden, ties a rope round a branch, and then, as she at last realizes what he is doing, loops the other end round his neck and jumps (another real case in my experience)? How can one assess the impact of something like this on the candidate's performance a day later?

In cases such as these it is very tempting to give the candidate whatever extra marks are necessary to achieve at least the forecast grade. This temptation must be resisted. It remains essential to award the 'right' result, for two very good reasons. First, it does a candidate no favours to award an undeserved grade. The same considerations apply as those described earlier in the case of a candidate who has missed part of the course. If the candidate moves on to a further course or career for which he is not fitted, but encouraged by a sympathetically inflated result, he may suffer a worse setback in the long run. Second, and especially when qualification for university is concerned, the disadvantaged candidate is not the only one in the equation. If he does not obtain the university place someone else will, and if he does someone else will be deprived. However sympathetic one may feel towards a particular identified candidate, with whom one can perhaps empathize, one must not forget the other candidate affected. There is no means of knowing who that candidate is; it takes a mental effort to remember that that candidate exists somewhere. Nevertheless, equity demands that although every consideration should be given to a disadvantaged candidate, it must not be inflated beyond what the evidence can justify.

For most of my years of experience in examining, the concession to be made to a temporarily handicapped candidate was in the hands of the grade review team. It was accepted that these people alone had the subject-specific expertise needed to judge what effect the particular handicap would have had in their subject. Nor were they required to make the decision in terms of a precise mark. If they were satisfied that without the handicap the candidate would have achieved a higher grade, the higher grade would be awarded without the need to add marks artificially.

This system, unfortunately, began to attract criticism because it was felt that the concessions given were not consistent from subject to subject. If three examining teams separately made decisions, each in their own subject, about the same candidate, those decisions might differ. I was never myself persuaded of the validity of this criticism; in fact what was being criticized seemed to me to be only what one would expect. If, for instance, a candidate had broken the wrist of her writing hand she would be seriously handicapped in a three-hour essay paper, but probably not handicapped at all in a multiple-choice paper which is answered by ticking boxes. Differences from subject to subject might be expected, and could well be right. However, Boards have begun to organize special consideration for such candidates by a dedicated team, not necessarily involving subject expertise, who will deal with all the candidates in all the subjects. This will certainly have the merit of consistency, if merit it be.

The growth of modular syllabuses has also had an impact, to me regrettable, on this process. When a candidate has taken a module prior to the final session, and was suffering from a handicap, the result must be issued in terms of a precise mark. He wishes to know what mark he is carrying forward and whether it would be wise to re-take the module. It will not do to defer consideration until the course is completed, all modules are taken, and one can see with fullest evidence what concession is appropriate. Someone must put an exact value on the candidate's handicap. To be realistic, this is impossible. One might know that the candidate would have done better without the handicap, and if he is quite close to a grade boundary one might be satisfied that he would have reached the higher grade. But would he have scored five more marks, or six, or seven? Who can say? Yet in modular syllabuses one *must* say. For this reason the Boards are evolving a fixed tariff system. Those processing these applications will now increasingly simply look up the handicap, read off the concession allocated to it, and add that mark to the candidate's score.

In reality, of course, any two candidates suffering from the same handicap might react quite differently. A most striking case of this is candidates suffering from bereavement. I have seen many whose father or mother has recently died who have actually surpassed their forecast grade in the examination. There are some who seem to brace themselves in the face of such a tragedy, who perhaps give of their best as if to do something that the parent would have wanted. Others of course disintegrate and fall far short of expectation. Until recently (but I sincerely hope no longer) some Boards followed a procedure whereby candidates with a temporary handicap were given an extra 10% of the marks *which they had actually scored*. To me this was the opposite of what is logical. If a candidate whose father had died scored 80% he could be given 88%. Yet it is clear that he has coped with the tragedy. On the other hand a similar candidate scoring 20% could only be given 22%, although it is apparent that he has been demoralized and is the one who needs the greater concession. At least a fixed tariff system, whatever its other deficiencies, overcomes this.

If candidates suffering from temporary handicap are to be assessed professionally, all the evidence should be fully considered. This will include the forecast grade, to be seen in the light of the Centre's accuracy in forecasting the grades of the other candidates, the performance of other candidates identified by the Centre as comparable with the handicapped candidate, and the candidate's actual performance. Some will be seen to have coped well with the handicap, and few extra marks, if any, will be justified; others might rightly deserve a significant addition. I am personally of the opinion that only subject specialists, the grade review team in fact, are fully qualified to make these decisions.

ADMINISTRATIVE ERRORS

Apart from their own personal and medical problems, candidates can be the victims of all sorts of administrative errors. It may be rash to say that these are *always* resolved in the best interest of the candidates, but that is certainly the intention of the Boards, whoever is responsible for the error. I used to believe that about seventy per cent of administrative errors were the responsibility of the Centres, not of the Boards. This was a guess, but I felt confidence in it. Recently the Boards may have made a higher proportion of errors, largely caused by the mergers of Boards, necessitating the amalgamation of diverse processing systems and staff dealing with unfamiliar systems and syllabuses. This will be rapidly overcome, no doubt. In Centres the key figure is the member of staff given the responsibility for administering the examinations. This will be a senior and experienced member of staff, who will still have to carry normal teaching and internal responsibilities. Organizing the examinations will be an additional part-time job with minimal training (perhaps a meeting once a year organized by the Board), such briefing as the previous holder of the post in the Centre is able to pass on, and in some cases a little clerical help. It is no surprise if people in this position make mistakes.

Examinations are highly complex. Each syllabus has its own identifying code (and there may be several syllabuses in the same subject); within each syllabus there may be a range of options, each with its own code. Each candidate has to have a personal candidate identifying number. The Centre may well enter with different Boards in different subjects, and although the Boards have worked hard in recent years to make their documentation uniform, differences still remain. The teachers of the separate subjects and the candidates themselves, who know the syllabus for which they have prepared and have to give that information to the Examinations Officer, are quite unaware of all the alternatives and may therefore overlook identifying details which are necessary. It is small wonder that mistakes are made.

CANDIDATES PREPARED FOR THE WRONG PAPER

Every year there will be cases of candidates opening the question paper only to find that it is one for which they have not been prepared. This may well be because they sent in a wrong syllabus or option code on the entry form. My own Board was once pilloried in the local press when a group of candidates found themselves in this position (the father of one of the candidates happened to work for the local paper). No apology was ever published, although we were able to show that they had been sent exactly what they had asked for. In fact nowadays this particular problem can be solved quickly thanks to the fact that nearly all Centres have a fax machine and a good photocopier. A telephone call to the Board to explain the situation will see the paper faxed through, and they can photocopy the number of papers required. The candidates will not be kept waiting long.

More embarrassing for the Centre, and more difficult to resolve, is when the candidates have been taught for the wrong syllabus. Every year there are several cases of this, in syllabuses with a fixed structure but a change of prescribed reading. This can easily happen in English Literature, Modern Languages and Classics, where the texts to be read change from year to year. My own Board's A-Level Religious Studies syllabus used to rotate the Synoptic Gospels, and more often than not someone somewhere would prepare candidates for the wrong Gospel. This mistake is made because at least three syllabus booklets, covering different years, are in the hands of teachers at any one time. Since courses last for two years they will have the booklets covering the two sets of candidates whom they are teaching, a third so that they can prepare for the next course to begin, and possibly a fourth if they have not thrown away the old one. It is not too difficult to teach from the wrong one, and the error may not be discovered until candidates prepared for an examination on, say, *Hamlet* open the question paper and find that it is on *Macbeth*.

Candidates in this predicament can take comfort in that it will almost always be possible to grade them. Their course will have been a valid one (in a different year it would have been the correct one) and at the least they can be graded on a part-absence basis. However, if at all possible, the Board is likely to provide a question paper on the material studied. This can be set at a later date, since there are no security implications, the new paper being unique to the Centre concerned.

CANDIDATES ENTERED WITH THE WRONG BOARD

Another error which I have met on a couple of occasions is to enter candidates with the wrong Board. If a Centre normally makes all its entries with one Board, but one department decides to be different, the Examinations Officer, if not properly briefed, will automatically put those entries with the usual Board. This may be discovered at the start of the examination and corrected easily by fax, but in a minority of subjects the papers of the two Boards might not be timetabled together. I met one case where the paper which the candidates should have taken had been sat by all the other Centres several days earlier. In that case the candidates were allowed to take the paper, and when the evidence was considered we concluded that no candidate showed any sign of having had prior knowledge of the questions. In fact we felt sure that if they had known that the paper had been taken elsewhere they would have complained to their teacher that they had missed the examination. Their failure to do so seemed to prove their honesty.

CANDIDATES NOT ENTERED

The oddest mistake which I have met was when a Centre failed to enter one of its candidates in one subject, and no one realized until the results were published and his name was not on the list in the subject concerned! This was in GCSE English Literature in the days when syllabuses consisting of 100 per cent coursework were still permitted. The candidate had done the work and it had been marked in the school. The school's work had been moderated by the sampling process, which meant that the absence of a candidate from the list could easily pass unnoticed. Since there was no written paper to take, when his arrival would have alerted the invigilator to the fact that his name was not on the list, the lack of entry remained undetected. Of course the solution was easy, since the work existed, had been marked, and had in effect been moderated as one of the total entry from the school. It was possible to issue a grade by return – and I suspect that the parents, who had been paying large fees to what is one of our most prestigious independent schools, never knew!

ERRORS IN CANDIDATE IDENTIFIERS

As usual, modular syllabuses have their own problem. Since candidates may spread their performances over several sessions it is essential that the identification of the candidates remains unchanged. Most Centres have now learned that they must always enter the candidates without changing the candidate numbers. However, I know that as recently as 1998 there have been Centres whose results would have shown, say, 60 candidates with two module results each, rather than twenty candidates with a full hand of six modules each. The Boards are aware of this and are usually able to resolve the problem before the results are published. If the problem applies to all a Centre's candidates it will be noticed and put right; but if it applies only to one candidate in a large group otherwise recorded correctly it is very likely to remain undetected until the results are published.

While the candidate number is crucial it is also desirable that the other identifying details are correct. A computer will assume that J. R. Smith, John R. Smith and J. Richard Smith are three different candidates. The best clue that they are not will be the date of birth – but I recall a case of twins given the same initials, some of whose results subsequently became confused. When parents name their children, examination entry details are the last thing they have in mind!

MALPRACTICE BY TEACHERS

While the above problems are outside the control of the candidates, they are quite capable of making problems for themselves by acts of malpractice, or more bluntly by cheating. Even teachers have been known to help candidates improperly, i.e. to cheat, and it is sad to say that instances of this are becoming more frequent. The recent emphasis on school league tables has introduced a competitive element in the teachers' minds. Headteachers are more likely to ask questions if results in a department are poor. Minority subjects which produce sub-standard results could find their place in the school curriculum under threat. Perhaps not surprisingly, teachers may go beyond what is permitted in order to protect their jobs. One cannot help but wonder if recent plans for higher pay for 'high flying' teachers will lead to more of this.

Teachers may give improper help in a number of ways: assistance with coursework, assistance in the examination room, interference with a script after it has been completed, and informing the candidates of the contents of the question paper in advance of the examination. This last is in fact so unusual that I have only personally once met a case where I was convinced, and still am, that it had taken place, although we were unable to prove it. It can only be done by, or with the collusion of, the Examinations Officer in the Centre, since the question papers when received from the Board have to be kept under lock and key in high security, and can only legitimately be opened in the examination room itself when they are to be handed out. The Boards carry out spot checks from time to time, and if a packet were found to have been opened the Centre might well be struck off the list of recognized examination centres, and so be unable to enter candidates. The risk is high, but it is not impossible that a desperate teacher might decide to take the chance.

Interference with a script is also unusual, something which I have met twice. When the examination is finished the scripts will be in the possession, briefly, of a member of staff, either one of the invigilators who has collected them and is to arrange them for posting to the examiner, or the Examinations Officer. If that teacher has a personal interest in one or more of the candidates it is no doubt tempting to have a quick look at the scripts. It is then tempting too to correct glaringly bad mistakes. On both the occasions when I met this offence the changes were unmistakable; the examiner who marked the script reported to the Board that there were corrections made to it in handwriting not that of the candidate, and reference back to the Centre quickly revealed what had happened. Two teachers lost their jobs, and probably their careers.

Giving assistance in the examination room itself is only possible if there is a lone invigilator. If there are fewer than 30 candidates it is permissible, though in my view very unwise, for there to be only one invigilator (provided that there are good arrangements in place to summon aid quickly in case of emergency, such as a candidate being taken ill). According to the regulations, that invigilator must have had no personal involvement with the candidates being invigilated, i.e. must not have taught them during the year leading up to the examination, and of course must not be related to any of them. However, Centres are sometimes lax about this, especially for winter sessions, when, unlike during the main session in the summer, the whole Centre is not in examination mode, and it may be convenient to try to fit in invigilation of a small group of candidates without disrupting the normal timetable of the rest of the pupils and teachers.

A teacher who helps in this way puts her career into the hands of the candidates. If she helps some but not all, those not helped will almost certainly report what has happened. If she helps all, one or two may well tell other pupils not involved in the examination, and so word gets back to authority. I have even met a case where the whole group of candidates helped were so worried about what had happened (whether from moral scruples or because they were afraid that they might all be disqualified I am not sure) that they went in a body to the Head of Centre to report it. Another career was brought to an abrupt end.

The easiest situation for giving this sort of help is at a language oral, when the invigilator doubles as the examiner, must be a specialist in the subject, and is in a one-to-one situation with the candidate. Since the oral examination is recorded, and the tape sent to an examiner of the Board for checking and/or marking, any improper help is often betrayed by what is on the tape. Obviously, skilful use of the pause button by the examiner may make it possible to avoid give-away details on the tape, and one cannot help wondering how often malpractice takes place undetected, but sufficient cases are proved to warn others who may be tempted that the risk is not sensibly worth taking. The most amusing case known to me involved a candidate for GCSE French being asked to name a place to go to for a day out. After a pause and some rustling of paper he said, 'Le Deux Cent'. There was a longer pause, and more rustling, after which he said, 'Ah, no, le Zoo'. Clearly the teacher had been writing down answers for him to read, but he had misread ZOO as 200!

IMPROPER HELP IN COURSEWORK

In coursework it is much more difficult to define what constitutes legitimate help and what does not. No candidate can attempt coursework untaught. The teacher must assist the candidate in choosing the topic, identifying suitable sources of information, and planning the structure of the work. If during the work the candidate needs help in these areas, for instance in finding further source material to follow up a point, or in re-angling the topic if it is not working well, the teacher can legitimately answer questions and give pointers. The teacher must also exercise sufficient supervision of the work to be satisfied that it is the candidate's own, that it is not being done by a friend or relative at home, or being copied verbatim from a book. This can only be done by looking at the work frequently, and probably by requiring some of it to be written up in class time under direct supervision. This will inevitably stir temptation to give more aid than is allowed, from a simple correction of spelling mistakes on the one hand to major corrections of fact or detailed suggestions for additional paragraphs on the other. This must not be done.

Cases have been reported to the Boards, and proved, where a teacher has collected in and marked a completed piece of coursework, and has handed it back to the candidate with instructions to re-write it incorporating all the corrections and suggested amendments. (I recall a candidate's mother telephoning the Board to say that this was being done for her son and to check that it was legitimate!) In practical subjects such as CDT there have been cases of a teacher doing some of the construction work for the candidates. I recall a case where the Board's moderator was to visit the Centre on a Monday morning, and at the end of the preceding Friday many of the candidates had not completed their constructions. Over the weekend the teacher completed all the work himself, only to be betrayed by the very pupils whom he was trying to help. They took one look at the models they were presenting to the moderator and declared them not to be their own!

I have even met a case where marks were submitted for coursework which had not been done! This is extraordinarily rash, since the Boards always send for a sample of work (choosing the sample themselves) in order to moderate the Centre's marking. At that point it becomes very obvious if the work does not exist at all. Teachers who make these mistakes are normally doing it from the best of motives: it is their fault that the work is incomplete or not even begun, because they did not organize the working time correctly, or did not brief their pupils correctly; they are trying to make it possible for their pupils to get the result which they are sure they deserve. Nevertheless, malpractice of this sort will almost inevitably cause loss of job and career.

PLAGIARISM IN COURSEWORK

If teachers occasionally succumb to the temptation to help the candidates improperly, how much more likely is it that the candidates themselves will attempt to cheat? The two commonest forms of cheating are plagiarism in coursework and attempting to smuggle helpful notes into the examination room.

It must be admitted that it is not easy to draw a line to distinguish plagiarism in coursework from legitimate research. No candidate can produce a piece of written coursework (one must make a distinction here with art and craft work) without reference to sources.

But the work submitted must clearly have passed through the candidate's own brain. Direct quotations must be put into quotation marks and acknowledged. If the submitted work consists of virtually nothing but acknowledged quotations it probably will not earn much credit, but the possibility will be there of reward for the selection of the quotations and their arrangement to construct an argument. On the other hand, unacknowledged quotations amount to an attempt to pass off someone else's work as the candidate's own. This is dishonest, i.e. cheating, and will at the very least lead to an award of no marks for the coursework, and could lead to disqualification in the subject.

Every year a good number of candidates are detected in plagiarism of this sort, but it must be admitted that one can have no idea how many remain undetected. It depends upon the vigilance and awareness of the teacher in the Centre and the moderator from the Board who checks the work (and since coursework is moderated by sample, the sheer volume precluding a full check, much coursework is never seen by anyone other than a teacher in the Centre). It may well be a matter of luck whether the teacher or moderator recognizes the quoted material, or identifies a style of English clearly not that of the candidate and so, realizing that there must be a published source, is able to track it down. I recall a case of a moderator feeling that a lengthy passage in a candidate's History coursework was impressive and familiar, and suddenly realizing that it came verbatim from a book which she herself had written! Bad luck, that candidate. I recall another case of a GCSE English Literature moderator being presented with an 'original' poem, only to see it framed on the wall of a hotel where she went on holiday. Again bad luck, that candidate. Music is another subject which tempts candidates to plagiarism in the composition element of the coursework. Frequently candidates submit compositions which they have 'borrowed' from distinguished composers. When the passages 'borrowed' may be only sixteen or twenty bars I am always impressed by the perception of the moderators who identify them.

Because there is inevitably an element of chance in detection of this type of cheating, Examining Boards are always going to be hard on it. Their only hope of preventing it is to make the penalties so severe, and known to be so severe, that candidates will know that it is too great a risk to take.

A second form of plagiarism, and one unlikely to be spotted by the moderator, is to submit another candidate's work as one's own, or to have one's work done by a relative or friend. The increasing use of computers to produce coursework (perfectly good in itself) has made it easier for one candidate to locate and print out the work of another, and this is happening with increasing frequency. Normally, of course, the teachers in the Centre identify this, because they will be presented with two identical or largely identical pieces of work. However, if a candidate were able to steal a piece of work submitted by another in the previous year the theft might well remain unnoticed.

It will be even harder to convict a candidate of having the work done by a parent outside school. I have met cases where the Centre was sure that the work was not the candidate's own, but faced with stout denials of dishonesty – and possibly threats of legal action from an outraged parent – the Centre has felt obliged to give way. If a Centre does not authenticate a piece of work as the candidate's own the Board will not accept the work. The Board itself has no means of knowing whether the work submitted is typical of that candidate, but can only rely on the Centre. That is why it is so important for Centres to keep a close eye on the production of all coursework, to ensure that at least some of it is produced under supervision, and to check on a regular basis the notes which candidates make in their own time. If the candidate is merely set the task and told to produce it three months later, the final version could have been produced by anyone, and if a word processor is used it might not even have been typed out by the candidate.

In this connection, if one candidate submits the work of another, the second candidate also has questions to answer. A candidate who colludes in this form of cheating is equally liable to be penalized, normally by the award of no marks for the component, but again potentially with disqualification in the subject. Candidates can easily be persuaded by a friend to lend their coursework: 'I only want to look at it, to see how to go about it and to get a few ideas'. The candidate who lends work in such circumstances, while certainly not expecting it to be copied, is still liable to penalty. This is exactly parallel to a candidate in the examination room who knowingly allows his script to be seen by the candidate in the next desk. No one would challenge disqualification in such circumstances. Similarly, a piece of coursework is in effect an examination script and so far as possible should be treated as such.

CHEATING IN THE EXAMINATION ROOM

The second common offence is to take notes into the examination room. This is almost inevitably a disqualification offence. Candidates plead forgetfulness: 'I was revising, put the notes in my pocket and forgot they were there'. However, the *Instructions for the Conduct of Examinations*, which is a booklet all Centres are required to follow, puts upon the invigilator at the start of the examination the obligation of reminding the candidates that any unauthorized material must be handed in. Forgetfulness is no defence.

An even feebler defence, though often offered, is to claim that the notes were not used and were in fact of no use. Obviously candidates do not know what questions will appear on the question paper, and so may well dishonestly take in material which turns out to be of no value. But what counts is the intention. A burglar caught in someone's house could not argue that he has done nothing wrong because he found nothing worth stealing. No more can a candidate claim innocence if illicit material is not used. The offence is simply that of having the material.

PENALTIES FOR CHEATING

Before modular syllabuses became common the penalty for an offence committed in one component was disqualification in the syllabus. In extreme cases this could be extended to cover all syllabuses which a candidate had entered in the session, or even a ban on entering examinations for a number of years. This last would be likely to be imposed upon candidates who committed a particularly heinous offence, such as burgling the safe at the Centre to steal copies of the question paper (which I know of happening twice), or arranging for impersonation so that someone else could take the candidate's place in the examination room (which is probably detected two or three times a year at Open Centres, where the candidates expect not to be known to the invigilators).

Disqualification from more than one syllabus could be the penalty for a candidate caught cheating a second time, or for a candidate deliberately plotting to take illicit advantage of a timetable change. When some candidates have taken an examination and others have not, there is always scope for a cunning candidate to collude with one who has already taken that question paper. Of course there will be supervision, but it is very hard for it to be perfect; one cannot accompany a candidate into a toilet cubicle, for instance (although one could search it before the candidate uses it!). I recall a candidate perfectly reasonably asking to get a book from his locker in order to revise for the coming examination. However, he had lent a key of the locker to a friend who would have previously taken the examination. The friend had put a piece of paper on which he had written details of the questions in the very book which the candidate took out. The supervising teacher was alert enough to check the book and both candidates found themselves with no A-Level grades that summer.

Modular examinations have created a problem in achieving equal penalties for all candidates who cheat. If a candidate is taking a single module in an early session, intending to carry the result forward to be aggregated with later modules, disqualification in the module is a relatively minor penalty. The module can be re-taken at a later session, just as it could have been if the original result, honestly achieved, had been disappointing. Yet it would be an extreme reaction for the Board to ban the candidate from a re-sit, and I do not know of this happening. Current practice when cheating is detected in a module is to disqualify the candidate in all modules being taken in that subject at that session. Clearly this is not equitable across all the candidates, since some will be taking more modules than others, and for those disqualified in their final session, when they had intended to aggregate the marks and obtain a syllabus grade, it is much more serious than for those disqualified in an earlier session, who have time to re-take and still obtain a syllabus grade at the intended time.

It is not easily practicable to disqualify in a module retrospectively, although in appropriate circumstances it can be done. A candidate who cheats when re-sitting a module may have considered the risk worth taking, since there will still be the earlier result to use when aggregating at syllabus level if the re-sit is disqualified. In such circumstances the Board can very reasonably disqualify retrospectively and expunge the earlier mark from its own records. If the candidate wishes to obtain a syllabus grade a further re-sit of that module will become necessary. On the other hand, the Board can hardly recover the evidence of the earlier result which is already in the possession of the candidate. (We don't live in a world where the heavies can be sent round to demand it back!) The candidate could presumably concoct a plausible story for not having completed the course, and present evidence of the earlier module result in applying for a job.

In the area of dealing with candidates who indulge in malpractice in modular examinations the Boards are still evolving their procedures. It is essential to be uncompromisingly firm if examinations are to retain public credibility; it may be impossible to achieve perfect equity.

VARIOUS MISHAPS

Apart from candidates who are handicapped and candidates who cheat, there seems to be no end to problems which can affect examinations. 'If it can happen it will happen, somewhere, to somebody.' Electric failures plunging the examination room into darkness, workmen drilling up the road outside with a din precluding rational thought, a candidate being violently sick on the floor to the dismay and distraction of the rest, the fire alarm ringing, a disaffected candidate wilfully misbehaving and distracting the others, are the sort of things which can and have all happened. In such cases the Centre is expected to use its common sense in order to complete the examination. The candidates may be moved to another room, closely supervised to prevent their talking to one another; an allocation of extra time to compensate for time lost in any disturbance will have to be judged. The Board will require a fully detailed report. The scripts will be marked as presented, and in the light of all the evidence the Board will decide whether any adjustments to the marks would be justified. The best interests of the candidates will be uppermost in the minds of those dealing with the problem. As in all the work of the Examining Boards in all subjects, the aim above all others is to award the 'right' results. That is the sole justification of the Boards' existence.

Chapter 8

The Evolving Examination Process and Future Possibilities

Since the mid-'80s the examining system has been in a state of flux, and there is little evidence that this is slowing down. 1988 saw the first examination for GCSE, which had replaced the dual system of O Level and CSE. Its purpose was to remove what had been seen to be the iniquity of dividing the candidates at an early age into passes and failures: the able took O Level; those deemed less able, perhaps as early as aged 14 if they made the choice at the beginning of a two-year course, settled for CSE. Grade 1 at CSE was officially considered the equivalent of an O-Level grade C, but it is not clear that all users regarded it as such.

TIERING IN GCSE

GCSE was hailed as a single system, and so it was up to a point: all candidates followed the same course. But even from the first some subjects were given a tiered structure. These were Mathematics, the Science subjects and Modern Languages. In these subjects it was necessary for candidates to decide at some stage whether it was realistic to sit the higher-tier papers or more sensible to forgo the possibility of the highest grades and so to offer the basic tier. Each tier was strictly controlled in the grades which could be gained through it. A candidate offering the higher tier who fell a single mark short of the lowest grade available on it would obtain no result, in common parlance a failure. On the other hand, a candidate entering for the basic tier who in the event scored 100% could not be awarded a grade above the ceiling for the tier, however certain one might have felt that the candidate had been wrongly entered at the lower level and was worth something more.

Since 1988 the syllabuses have all been revised and a tiered structure has become the norm. Those now exempt from tiering are a very small minority indeed for which some sort of special case has been made in terms of the inherent nature of the subject. In effect the old O-Level/CSE divide has been reintroduced by the back door. What has been gained is easy transferability from one tier to the other. Although the entry must be made about four months before the examination is sat, the candidate may still change tier up to the very moment of entering the examination room. Some subjects, notably Modern Languages, have a more helpful use of the tiered system by requiring all the candidates to take the basic tier, after which they may stop, or move on to the intermediate tier, and then again have the choice of stopping or going on. In 1998 the grades available on the higher tier were also extended by one, not indeed by a full grade band, but by allowing those with a very near miss to be given the next grade down.

All this is an attempt to reconcile human considerations on the one hand with examining theory on the other. It is very difficult to set a question paper which is a fair test for candidates right across the ability range from A* to G. If there are questions sufficiently demanding to allow the A* candidate to show that level of ability, they will be quite impossible for the G-grade candidate, who will leave the examination in a state of frustration. But if some of the questions are right for G-level ability the A* candidate will find them trivial and a waste of time. The G-grade candidate should not be given that grade for a bad performance on hard questions. The scraping up of a mark or two here and there is little more than a lottery, does not give the Grading Committee any worthwhile evidence on which to make proper decisions, and so allows no proper distinction between F, G and unclassified. Nor should the

A* candidate earn that grade by a faultless performance on a lot of easy questions; if that level of award is to be made there must be sufficient quality evidence in response to questions of that standard to demonstrate its justification. At the end of the examination every candidate must emerge with a sense of having faced a fair test in which he has been able properly to demonstrate his level of ability.

In some few subjects one tier of examination allows this possibility. In Art and similar craft subjects, for instance, the candidates will each paint or make something at their own level of ability without the need to set them different levels of task. In coursework it is generally accepted in most subjects that candidates will undertake for themselves tasks at their own level of ability. History very quickly developed the theory of 'levels of response' marking, whereby common questions could be set which would allow candidates to respond with varying levels of understanding and analysis. The historians made this case so convincingly that, surprisingly, they are one of the subjects now exempt from the need for tiers. One might have thought that what was acceptable for History might have held good for English too, but that case has not yet been made.

The situation is still evolving, and more subjects may lose their tiered structure. Greek, for instance, is about to do so, certainly not because it is fitted for a single examination across the ability range (quite the reverse) but simply because it is a selective subject which only the most able study. If there are virtually no candidates for the lower tier it is a waste of resources to set one. It is encouraging to see that flexibility is being allowed in the system, that subjects may be allowed to have one tier, two or three according to their own character, and that there has been an easing, however small, in the restriction on the grades which may be awarded to those with a near miss. At this level we have a reasonable structure only in need of fine tuning subject by subject.

THE ORIGINAL CONCEPT OF AS

AS and A Level are at a different stage, with their big shake-up about to come. Once again one cannot help fearing that we shall begin with a rigid structure, so beloved of planners, into which flexibility will be introduced over time, as has happened with GCSE. The fact that individual subjects have their own characteristics which syllabuses should be allowed to acknowledge is rarely recognized until the weaknesses of what is imposed have become clear in practice. We shall also have to learn to refer to 'specifications' instead of syllabuses, but the word 'syllabus' will be used for the remainder of this chapter, as being the word which will more naturally be understood by readers.

AS was first examined in 1989. Its very worthy aspiration was to widen the curriculum and overcome the educational restrictions of over-specialization too early. The hope was that the specialist scientist would take one or two humanities or languages at AS, while the English, History or languages specialist would similarly take AS in one or two contrasting subjects. This did not happen. With very few honourable exceptions schools did not find it practicable to make timetable provision for AS teaching. When candidates ventured upon AS they were more likely to add a subject in their own field rather than one which contrasted, or perhaps they dropped from three full A Levels to two, in order to take one AS (a reduction in what they had been doing!) or two but with no increased demand upon their timetable.

In some subjects (and probably most) the concept of AS as half an A Level in terms of half the content but studied at full A-Level standard was inherently flawed. In a language, for instance, one simply cannot reach the full standard in half the study time. On the surface one can drop, for instance, that part of the syllabus consisting of prescribed literature, but a candidate would naturally become a better linguist, with a wider vocabulary and more familiarity with the language, by reading such books, and will therefore be better fitted for the half of the subject retained for AS assessment. In most subjects one part impacts upon another, even if this is not obvious. A candidate who has studied Shakespeare will have developed skills of literary criticism and appreciation which will enrich study of twentieth-century literature; a student of British history will gain a grasp of historical concepts helpful in studying European history. Candidates who have not studied the full course will be less well fitted for that part which they have studied. For this reason candidates and teachers alike quickly realized that AS was more than half A Level, and this was another reason why they were reluctant to tackle it.

THE NEW AS FROM SEPTEMBER 2000

The failure of this system, and the basic illogicality of it, has been recognized, and in September 2000 teaching will begin for a revised structure. In this, AS will be the first half of the A-Level course and will be pitched at the standard to be expected of candidates halfway through a full course. Yes, the standard of AS will have been reduced (and one wonders why the change is not made clearer by giving it a different name; something as simple as SA might help) but this need not matter if A Level is not adversely affected. We may indeed have gained an examination and a qualification which will attract those who feel that the full A Level is beyond them and who at present leave education after GCSE. But will the new approach meet the original intention of encouraging A-Level students to broaden the range of subjects which they study?

Here, I think, we shall be no better off than we were before, and again timetable considerations are at the root of the problem. Most schools allow eight periods per week for study of an A-Level subject, so that candidates attempting three A Levels are committed to 24 periods of taught study. There will be perhaps a dozen more in total for private study in school time, and for the range of highly beneficial but unexamined activities which many schools think it desirable to include: activities of cultural, moral and physical education. At present a candidate offering an AS must commit four periods per week for the two years of the course, or could give up an A Level and replace it with two AS subjects with no loss of time at all. But when AS becomes the full first year of the A-Level course, however sensible on other grounds that may be, a candidate adding an AS to three A Levels will commit 32 periods in the week to taught study, and it will actually be impossible to add two AS subjects to the normal three studied for A Level. This will be less attractive than the system which it replaces.

It is true that the candidate will complete AS study in the first year of the course, and the timetable in the second year will recover the periods of unexamined study lost. It is also true that a candidate could take one AS subject in the first year of the course and another in the second, but this would require her to work with the pupils a year behind for that second AS, which may not be psychologically appealing, and could well be impossible in timetabling terms: she would have to be free in the second-year timetable for the very periods which coincided with the teaching to the first-year students of the subject which she wanted to take. My guess is that the new system will be less successful in terms of increasing the appeal of AS to the normal A-Level candidature, although it might attract candidates not intending to go on to the full A Level, some of whom may be sufficiently successful in fact to do so.

Whether statistics will ever emerge to enable us to find out what the impact of the new AS will have been remains to be seen. The statistics at present published for AS are of course simply a record of those candidates who took a subject without going on to the full A Level. Future statistics will show a vastly increased number of candidates for AS, since they will include all those who are going on to the next stage. The figures will only be meaningful if they can separate those who stop at that point from those who go on to A Level, and this will be impossible until at least a year later when one can see who has gone on and who has not. We must beware of the planners of the new system trumpeting their own success by failing to make this vital distinction.

THE IMPACT OF THE NEW AS ON A-LEVEL STANDARDS

What about the impact upon the A-Level standard? In this system, since AS will be the first half of the A-Level assessment and will contribute 50% of the marks to the final A-Level grade, it appears to be acknowledged that half of the A Level will be of a lower standard than it was before. The reality will vary from subject to subject and will only be fully appreciated by subject specialists in each case. It is a mistake to suppose that there is some absolute A-Level standard which is met by every question on every examination paper in every subject. It is a perfectly respectable, and indeed recommended, approach to have an incline of difficulty over the questions on a paper, beginning with a relatively easy starter but ending with something really complex and taxing. In some cases parts of the subject are inherently easier than others; for instance, as a classicist I should say that translating unprepared Latin prose into English is easier than doing the same for Latin poetry, and I feel sure that most classicists would agree. Probably most subjects have their easier and harder elements. In Mathematics, which pioneered modular syllabuses, there is a sequence in the modules, as the later build upon the earlier, and could presumably not be done without the earlier ones as a foundation. In fact for many years Mathematics has offered two A-Level qualifications: Mathematics and Further Mathematics. Only the very best mathematicians have also attempted Further Mathematics, and even then many of them have fallen a grade or two down in the latter compared with their Mathematics grade. It seemed inescapable that the two syllabuses, both officially A Levels, were of a different standard.

More recently the distinction has been blurred under the modular system. With six modules required for an A Level, a candidate taking twelve Mathematics modules can be awarded an A-Level grade in both Mathematics and Further Mathematics. Moreover, with only minor limitations, he can combine the twelve module results into two groups of six in the most convenient way. A candidate with 100% on six modules and 60% on the other six would combine three of those scoring 100 with three scoring 60, to give a total of 480 and an A grade (by the UMS scale; see Chapter 3) and similarly with the other six modules, rather than accept grade A for 6 × 100 and grade C for 6 × 60. All modules are treated as being of equal difficulty, even if they are not.

If the new AS consists of material which would have appeared as the easier parts of the old A-Level examination, the full A-Level assessment will not be watered down. In some subjects this may be possible, in others not. Examinations assess both content and skills. However, it is not easy to separate the two; skills have to be exercised upon content, not in isolation from it. Thus, to take an example, a candidate in History must know what happened, the content, and must display skills of analysis and evaluation in understanding and explaining the causes and consequences of what happened and in assessing the relative merits and reliability of the different sources. Of course it would be possible simply to learn what happened for AS, and to be examined on knowledge, and to develop the skills for assessment a year later at A Level. But this is not the realistic way in which History is normally taught. Candidates analyse and evaluate in parallel with learning the material. They are more likely both to cover and to analyse one chronological period, or the history of one part of the world, in the first year of the course and another in the second. The two years will expect the same standard of achievement. It is true that if an examination were set at the end of the first year the candidate is not likely to perform as well as at the end of two. Maturity is a factor; a further year's study will have deepened understanding and sharpened perception. Nevertheless, neither teaching nor examining has made any concessions to that. In future it will either have to make such concessions, with less demanding examination papers for AS, or to distort the teaching in subjects such as History by artificially separating the material into easier elements for examination after one year and harder after two.

However the different subjects try to cope with this problem, the key to the maintaining of standards ought to lie in the final grading decisions. It could remain in the hands of Grading Committees to counterbalance easier papers by setting more demanding grade boundaries, if they are left free to do so. On the other hand, the aggregation rules for modular syllabuses will in practice make this difficult. The AS-grade boundaries will have to be set realistically for an examination at the halfway point in the course, if only to be fair to those candidates for whom AS is their highest ambition and who will stop at that point. Yet every module will carry equal weight in the final assessment, and the conversion of the boundaries onto the UMS scale will ensure this. Of course Grading Committees could then set boundaries higher than those currently expected at A Level on the modules which make up the second half of the assessment, to offset the lower standard of the early modules, but I do not see this as realistic or fair. The Grading Committee, whose experience enables them confidently to set boundaries to established standards, would be attempting both to identify that standard and then to move the line to some notional point above it. With what confidence and by what criteria could this be done? My guess is that the top grades will become easier to get as half of the assessment contributing to them will be less demanding.

LIKELY ENTRY POLICY FOR THE NEW AS

Another feature of the intended assessment which could well further this trend arises from the rules governing the taking of the AS papers. They are of course designed to be taken at the end of the first year of the course, and their standard will be appropriate to that, but candidates are perfectly free to defer this and to take them after two years, along with the full A-Level papers, if they so wish. It seems to me virtually certain that candidates will produce a better result after two years of study than after one. For instance, to choose a very obvious example, a candidate in oral French will inevitably be more confident and fluent after a further year of speaking the language. If the AS papers are broadly being taken by candidates for whom they were not intended, the results will become distorted. The boundaries will obviously have to be set correctly, in order not to penalize unfairly candidates who take the papers at the intended time, nor would it be practicable (and probably not sensible) to try to have different boundaries for different categories of candidate: those taking the papers after one year of study and those taking them after two. But this will leave the results very difficult to interpret.

There may well be pressure upon candidates to take AS after one year of the course, particularly from universities. If admissions tutors begin to put weight upon AS results in making conditional offers of places, as they well may do since these results will appear to give them current and concrete evidence of the applicant's attainment, many candidates will take these papers after a year of study. But they will be fully at liberty to re-sit them and to improve their score a year later. I suspect that many will do so, and not simply because their first effort produced a disappointing result, but because even a good result can be improved. A candidate scoring 75% and a grade A on AS, who then receives a conditional offer requiring grade A at A Level for a university place, may well feel that the 75% could be improved to 80%, 85% or even more, and that perhaps little extra study, if any, would be necessary. To take the example of a French oral, already suggested, no extra work at all may be necessary in order to re-sit. In other subjects, if the area of content covered for AS is not being repeated for A Level, some work may be necessary to revise and retain the factual knowledge, but any skills to be deployed should be being developed through the areas of study being followed for A Level, and the extra demands for a re-sit of AS may be small enough to be acceptable.

I visualize the scenario of many candidates taking AS at the 'correct' time but re-sitting a year later, with improved results, and so producing an apparent, but not real, improvement in A-Level standards. To my mind the two levels of assessment are different and should be kept apart. One would not contemplate allowing candidates to carry GCSE marks forward to contribute to A-Level assessment, let alone to take GCSE papers in their A-Level year and use marks gained in them in that way. The flaws in allowing AS to be used in this way are less obvious, since we are accustomed to a system in which AS has been of the full A-Level standard. It will still be a part of the A-Level course, again helping to conceal the flaw in the system, but since it is of a different standard it creates both illogicality and practical difficulty in allowing it to contribute to the A-Level grade.

THE IMPACT OF THE NEW AS/A LEVEL ON THE TIMETABLE

This also has a serious impact upon the examination timetable, and consequently upon teaching in the schools. Since candidates may sit both AS and A Level in the same session they cannot be timetabled to take place simultaneously. It follows that the examination period will be longer. If the results are to be published in mid-August, as at present, there is no scope to let the timetable run later (the procedures and quality controls described in earlier chapters cannot be carried out in a shorter time) and so it will have to start earlier, perhaps quite early in May. But this in turn will cut off two or three weeks of teaching time. This is to be added to the fact that in the first year of the course candidates will have lost teaching time to take the AS examination. Indeed, if the AS question papers are timetabled before the A-Level papers, as seems natural and which accords with the standard practice of putting the easier material first in the examination, the AS course will be one of little more than two terms. At present schools almost certainly hold their own internal examinations for candidates halfway through the course, but these will normally be fitted into a single week well into June. Of course a scenario putting the AS papers into May and the A-Level papers into June would allow the AS candidates to put in a month of study after completing the AS papers, but this fragmentation of the course would hardly be beneficial to consistent study. Timetable considerations may not be the major factor in a candidate's deciding whether or not to sit the AS papers after one year, let alone, having done so, whether to re-sit a year later; but teachers will be very concerned as they plan their programme for the two years.

There is the additional factor that in modular syllabuses, which it appears that almost all will be, there will be an examination session in January. In view of the shortness of teaching time up to the summer session it may turn out that the January session will become popular for a first sitting of the AS papers, unless the pressure to take them comes from the universities, in which case January may be too late. It seems quite wrong that factors other than what is educationally best should decide these matters, and that teaching requirements seem to take second place to those of examining.

MODULAR AS AND A LEVELS

The previous paragraphs have been written on the assumption that each A-Level syllabus will consist of six components, or modules: three for stage one, AS, and three for stage two. This has been laid down as the requirement, although there is no doubt that some subjects do not welcome it and may strive (probably unsuccessfully until a few years' experience has proved them right) to obtain exemption from it. It is of course superficially attractive that all syllabuses should have a common structure. Quite apart from making module results easily understandable, it also opens up flexibility to use modules in different syllabuses. A candidate could take a couple of modules in, say, Physics, and then go on to combine them with four more modules in Physics, to obtain an A Level in that subject, or with two modules in Chemistry and two in Biology for an A Level in Science. Similarly in the fields of Economics, Business Studies and possibly Geography there may be modules which could be common to any. The range of vocational qualifications is also brought into play as, for instance, Travel and Tourism seems to have areas of relationship with Business Studies and Geography. No doubt there are many more attractive combinations too. But modules are only transferable if they are of equal value, as they will be required to be.

In order to achieve this there must be an anxiety that the structure of some syllabuses will be artificial, and that the need to create six modules will have an impact upon the standard required. For instance, there are syllabuses at present with four components. Breaking these up into six modules may not be easy and, especially if two new areas of study were to be added, the existing four might have to be reduced in demand to make room. Are six lighter topics of the same academic value as four more deeply studied? This is at least debatable. Let us take English Literature as an example. Four papers in different areas of literature has long been a common pattern. Clearly one could add two more on different areas of literature. The whole corpus of English literature can be divided in many ways: Shakespeare, the novel, twentieth-century literature, drama, poetry, Chaucer, feminist literature, and a host of other possible categories. It is not difficult to select six. But if the present Shakespeare paper, as one of four, demands the study of two plays in depth, it may be necessary to reduce this to one to allow room in the teaching time to study something in a new category. Will each category be as demanding as what has been replaced? Alternatively one could cut the original four papers to three, abandoning one area of study, but beef up the three survivors and set two papers, one AS and one A Level, on each of them. It is hard to say whether this is a better or worse solution. What seems wrong is that subject specialists will not be allowed to structure their syllabuses as they think best in terms of the inherent nature of the subject, but will be obliged to fit into a predetermined template. Mathematics and Art are different from each other; so are Physics and French; so are Music and Geography. It is not unreasonable to allow the pattern of assessment to reflect their differences.

Just as the tiered structure in GCSE has begun to gain flexibility, some subjects having one tier, some two and some three, so it may be that over time some subjects at A Level may gradually gain exemption from a six-module structure when it can be seen that this forces them into unnatural divisions of the subject. As a start, the concept of a double module (a single module carrying double weight) may be allowed to open the door.

If, in fact, modules are to become the cornerstone of the A-Level system, and if part of the purpose is to give them a semi-independence whereby one module may appear as an element in more than one syllabus, a natural extension of the process might be for them to become the basic qualification. Why should not a module stand in its own right? Why must a candidate take three (for AS) or six for A Level, rather than some other number? In Mathematics candidates quite often take more than the six modules which they need and discard the surplus weak results. Why cannot the discarded modules appear on the candidate's record?

At first sight this may appear to be a formula for the fragmentation of A Level. On the other hand, it might fit very well with the needs of candidates, especially the less able. A candidate who wished to read, say, Engineering at university would still take six modules in Mathematics, six in Physics, and either six in Chemistry or six more in Mathematics. In that case the change in the currency from syllabuses to modules would have made no difference in what was studied and examined. But those candidates all of whose three A-Level subjects are essential to their future intentions are relatively few. The aspiring student of English will clearly offer the full syllabus, six modules, in English. At present this is likely to be supported by two more full A Levels in what are seen as supporting subjects: History, a classical language, or a modern language, would be sensible. But how much more valuable it might be if the candidate could take a dozen modules spread over a range of subjects.

This would also cater for the candidate who is perhaps only capable of one A Level, or perhaps even none. Most teachers have met those who return to school in the sixth form to re-take a couple of GCSE subjects, and because they want to act in the school play or have a season in the First XI. The school usually puts them in for a full A Level or two (or AS now that it is available). But a course involving the basic modules in Mathematics and a Science, oral French, a chosen aspect of English Literature, and Twentieth-century British History might be useful, accurately reflect the candidate's interests and (limited) abilities, and give something of value to be presented to a prospective employer. It need not be a multiple of three or six if the results are to be recorded separately rather than in aggregation.

If this approach were adopted, it would of course throw into sharper focus the two levels within A Level. A full subject consists, by definition, of three AS and three A-Level modules. If results were recorded by the module they would naturally have to be labelled each to show its own level. In general, candidates taking single modules in different subjects would be likely to take AS modules only, but this need not be so. There is a good case for a candidate with a particular strength to pursue it at both levels, while ignoring other aspects of the subject. A candidate good at spoken French might well take the AS and A-Level oral modules, without attempting written French or French Literature. Perhaps this approach is one for our policy-makers to consider.

RESOURCE IMPLICATIONS OF THE NEW AS/A LEVEL

An inevitable consequence of the AS and A-Level reforms will be an increased cost in examining. There will be more question papers. These will have to be set, printed, marked, graded, and the results published. All these things cost money. Examiners have to be paid to set and mark, to attend meetings for standardization, grading and grade review. For most of them the fees (small as they are) are the basic motivation in doing the work. More paper in vast quantities will be consumed, more data-processing resources will be committed, more administration costs will be incurred. Added to the increased stress on the young people facing examinations, the reduction of teaching time (i.e. doing what education is all about) in the face of more examinations, and bearing in mind that examination results are not as definitive as so many take them to be (see Chapter 3), one cannot help wondering whether it is all worth it. Has the examination system got out of hand?

THE NUMBER OF EXAMINING BOARDS

Just as the examinations themselves are evolving, so too are the Examining Boards. Fifteen years ago there were seven GCE Boards in England plus one each in Wales and Northern Ireland (Scotland has a further Board with its own different system) offering A and O Levels. CSE was offered by Boards separate from the GCE Boards, regionally based and only entitled to accept entries from Centres in their geographical area. The vocational Boards were again quite separate, and the two sectors, academic and vocational, were hardly aware of one another.

When GCSE was introduced the Boards were grouped together to form four Examining Groups in England, while Wales and Northern Ireland (and of course Scotland, which did not adopt GCSE) remained separate. Each of the four Groups included both GCSE and CSE Boards. In practice these groupings of formerly independent Boards had to have a central management, which made it difficult for them to retain their individual independence. The GCE Boards in the partnership still had their A Levels, which were none of the Group's business, and so those Boards retained a foundation for independence. The CSE Boards had no further function other than as part of the Group, and very quickly found themselves taken over by one of their GCE partners. In effect they ceased to exist, although in many cases their offices remained open and their staff continued to be employed. The Southern Universities Joint Board (SUJB), the smallest of the GCE Boards, quickly found itself unable to survive on A-Level work and its share in the Midland Examining Group (MEG) alone, and was taken over by one of its larger partners, the University of Cambridge Local Examinations Syndicate (UCLES).

1995 saw a significant reduction in the number of Boards. It had always seemed illogical that the universities of Oxford and Cambridge should support three Examining Boards between them, UCLES (mentioned above), the University of Oxford Delegacy of Local Examinations (UODLE) and the Oxford and Cambridge

Schools Examination Board (OCSEB). Perhaps as surprising was that while UCLES and OCSEB were both in the Midland Examining Group, UODLE was a member of the Southern Examining Group (SEG), in partnership with the Associated Examining Board (AEB). The escalating costs of examination development, with an expensive complete re-write of the A-Level syllabuses just over the horizon, convinced Oxford University that it might soon find itself supporting money-losing bodies. Accordingly a merger of the three Boards was agreed, under the title of the Oxford and Cambridge Examinations and Assessment Council (OCEAC). UODLE, now part of OCEAC, had to detach itself gradually over the next couple of years from its involvement with SEG, since it was unacceptable for it to have a foot in two different GCSE Groups.

Meanwhile political pressure was growing both to reduce the number of Boards and syllabuses and to establish Boards which could offer a full assessment service, covering academic and vocational qualifications. The Government expressed its view that reduction to one Board was not appropriate, since it would leave Centres with no choice, but that the existing four A-Level Boards were too many. Two or three, then! However, there were three vocational Boards in existence, City and Guilds, BTEC and RSA, which seemed to dictate a three-Board solution.

BTEC and London were the first to merge, forming a single Board with the title EDEXCEL. OCEAC followed suit, combining with the RSA and changing its name yet again, this time to OCR, the letters representing the Oxford, Cambridge and RSA units in the partnership. This left the AEB to ally with the Northern Examinations and Assessment Board (NEAB) and City and Guilds, which they have done under the title of the Assessment and Qualifications Alliance (AQA).

POSSIBLE REDUCTION TO ONE BOARD

To the public in general it is a mystery why there cannot be a single Board. It would certainly put an end to allegations of varying standards, between Boards if not between subjects. It would set aside any suggestion of commercial competition in academic matters, which should be purely objective. On the other hand it might be a recipe for concealing inconsistencies of standard rather than for preventing them.

The key problem would be that of standardizing the marking. A number of small Boards meant that in any one syllabus the number of candidates, and therefore the number of examiners required, was not too big. Even in a large syllabus one Principal Examiner could standardize the Team Leaders, who could each standardize a team of eight or ten Assistant Examiners: the chain of command was not too long. But what if 1,000 examiners, or even more, were needed, as would be the case if there were only one syllabus in, say, GCSE English or Mathematics? The chain of command must be longer; the time required to complete the exercise must be much greater. How would the standardization meeting take place? Ideally all the examiners take part, have freedom to ask their questions about contentious points of marking and difficult judgemental decisions which they have found in their scripts, and can be checked as they carry out trial marking at the meeting. In a single mass meeting (would the Board hire the Albert Hall for the day?) not all could ask their questions and have their say. But if the Principal Examiner held the meeting with the Team Leaders only, and they then each held separate meetings with their teams, consistency across the examining teams could not be guaranteed. Inevitably new and different points would be raised in the different meetings, and differing decisions would possibly be taken. Similarly, as the marking proceeds, examiners often find a point in a script which the meeting did not cover. In such circumstances they telephone the Principal Examiner for a ruling. Quite apart from the danger of his having to spend days on end on the telephone receiving such calls, it is then necessary for such rulings to be disseminated quickly, normally again by telephone, to all the examiners, in case any of them come across the same point in their own marking. The practicalities are terrifying and leave great scope for failures of communication. And what if at some later stage in the process one of the Team Leaders were found to have been unsatisfactory? He would presumably, therefore, have been standardizing Assistant Team Leaders wrongly, and they in turn passing down a false standard to their teams. A large swathe of the examining team could have been applying mistaken judgements as information passed in a system like Chinese whispers from the top to the bottom. When detected, putting it right could take weeks of effort and re-marking. Almost certainly many errors and inconsistencies would remain undetected, while with only a single set of statistics and no other syllabus for comparison there would be no pointers to warn of these discrepancies.

THE NUMBER OF SYLLABUSES PER SUBJECT

It is worth considering also how many syllabuses are appropriate in any subject. A single Board offering many syllabuses would avoid the problems identified above, while simplifying administrative procedures by having only one management structure, but academically it would be no different from several Boards, each with a single syllabus. Over the years the Boards have been pilloried for what was considered to be an inordinate number of syllabuses. Was this fair? Every syllabus which existed was there to meet a need. Since each syllabus costs money to administer it would have been in the Boards' own interests to keep them to a minimum. But if a group of candidates were studying a subject from a particular aspect, with a particular educational philosophy, would it have been right to refuse to assess them, or to insist that they come back into the main stream? Could one legitimately insist that since the great majority of students in History study modern history there would be no syllabus in medieval history for those who preferred to study it? Since what the Boards are not prepared to assess will not be studied (so much for learning for its own sake, but in view of the importance of paper qualifications one has to be realistic) the Boards have it in their power to control what is taught in British schools. They could banish some parts of some subjects for ever. The only solution, which so far the Boards have honourably maintained to their own cost, has been to have several syllabuses, or a range of options within a syllabus.

This last possibility is important, since it raises the question of what a syllabus is. I used to claim, tongue in cheek, that my own Board found it possible to examine History at A Level by means of one syllabus, whereas other Boards had several. I did not add, because it did not suit my case, that we had over forty components, of which a candidate was required to attempt three. Although there were rules of combination to prevent a complete free-for-all, the number of possible combinations ran to several hundred. A critic could have argued that we had that many syllabuses.

In the case of History just quoted the range of options was at least explicit in the syllabus. In many subjects it is at least as great but not explicit. I am thinking particularly of subjects involving prescribed literature: English, Modern Languages and Classical Languages. A literature paper may well offer, say, six texts, of which candidates must choose two. In English Literature this may apply to several papers. Not only does this create a range of options, but when they exist within one and the same paper the marking and processing of the results normally has to be based on the assumption that they are all of exactly the same standard. If the questions on one book and the marking of it prove to have been severe or lenient it will not be easy to make any adjustment to allow for that. For instance, if the Shakespeare paper had questions on three plays and those set on, say, *King Lear* had proved difficult, it might be desirable to add five marks to every candidate who had answered on that play. But the computer would not know which candidates these were. Since obviously the problem would not be known before the marking began, it would not be possible to instruct the examiners to add an automatic five marks to each candidate who had made that choice. The only resource would be to go clerically through all the scripts at a late stage in the process to make the correction, and to delay the grading and grade review until it had been done.

A case can be made for allowing no alternative options in a syllabus. This would certainly make for more efficient and reliable examining. On the other hand, in the same way as reducing to a single syllabus, it would remove areas of study and some texts from education for ever. Many works of literature only remain in print because they are prescribed for examinations, thus guaranteeing their publishers sales sufficient to justify the printing. While obviously the sales of texts retained would rise, to the publishers' delight, those dropped would quickly fall out of print. The world of examining is only part of the educational process; it must remain aware of how its decisions impact upon related areas, of which publishing is one, and must accept its responsibility to them.

If there were to be one syllabus in each subject I wonder how it would be decided which one should survive? In the Sciences, for instance, there are three distinct and strong traditions: the Nuffield suite of syllabuses, the Salters suite, and the traditional suite which carries no distinguishing label. Each has its own vocal and convinced adherents. Each presents its own well-defined philosophy of the subject. Heaven help whoever tries to chair a meeting aimed at reducing them to one! It would be a blood-on-the-floor occasion. And what about Religious Studies? At present all the major world religions figure as options in a normal syllabus. Who would tell the Muslims, or the Jews, that their religion had been dropped?

My belief is that criticism of the number of syllabuses in any subject stems from prejudice. As a non-mathematician I cannot myself understand the need for more than one syllabus in Mathematics. I take Mathematics to cover a range of undebatable facts and concepts; $2 + 2 = 4$ and offers no variations. When a mathematician tries to explain the different philosophies of SMP and MEI my eyes glaze over; I can't follow. But if I know nothing about it, why should I assume that those who do are wrong? Then in turn I find it self-evident that there can be more than one syllabus in my own subjects, and am surprised that others cannot see that. They simply think I am empire building. No, the number of syllabuses must match the number of approaches to the subject. The number of options within a syllabus must match the range of content which that syllabus legitimately covers. Attempts to determine the number of syllabuses to be allowed on other grounds ('If you have over 10,000 candidates in the subject you can have a second syllabus') are doctrinaire and a negation of education, ruling out valid and valuable courses of study. Examining must be tailored to suit what is legitimately being taught, not vice versa. But whether this approach will find favour over the next decade must be very doubtful.

VOCATIONAL EXAMINATIONS

One aspect of the newly merged examining bodies is to put academic and vocational qualifications on a par. The latter, NVQ and GNVQ, have been pressed hard by policy-makers, but with limited success. 'Parity of esteem' is the target, but esteem cannot be awarded; it has to be earned. Since it depends upon what the users, and the public in general, feel about the qualification, we must have syllabuses which are seen to be as firmly based on knowledge and skills as their academic counterparts, and which are assessed as professionally and rigorously. Everything possible is being done to bring this about, and the incorporation of the vocational Boards into the traditionally respected academic Examining Boards, whereby common procedures can be established and the same quality controls put in place for all qualifications, can only help.

Ultimately what matters is what is taught and how well it is taught in schools. Just because new syllabuses become available it does not follow that schools will teach them: they can only teach what they have the staff to teach and resources to support. I expect vocational qualifications to make progress, but only slowly. The traditional top academic schools will not shed a subject currently in their curriculum to create a gap for a vocational subject, nor sack a teacher to be replaced by one with expertise in a new subject. There will be evolution if there is demand, from parents and from pupils. It may prove to be a vicious circle: low esteem, so little demand; little demand, so low esteem. On the other hand, schools with less academic candidates who have been searching for alternatives to A Level may take every opportunity to bring them in, and if they are successful there could be a widening swell of support. We shall see, but my guess is that wider acceptance and uptake of vocational qualifications within the normal school curriculum, while sure to come, will be a slow process.

POLITICAL INFLUENCE

Behind all educational development in recent years has been political pressure. It is only right and proper that governments should wish to ensure the best possible education for all our children – that is one of their functions. But politicians feel subject to a factor which does not fit with, and may disrupt, the normal tenor of educational progress: haste. A Secretary of State may well not be in office for more than two or three years, either being moved to a new post or because of an election. He or she will therefore want to see policies brought to fruition during his or her time in the post. But this is rarely possible. Examination courses run for two years before the examination itself is taken. Teachers are entitled to receive the full final syllabuses at least six months before the teaching starts, in order to ensure that they have the necessary books and resources, and to attend any training which the Examining Boards are providing nowadays as a normal part of their service. But before the syllabus can be issued it has to be written. This may even require a year or so while the QCA and the DfEE consult upon and write the criteria which will govern the syllabuses, before the Boards can begin writing the syllabuses themselves. The Boards are then likely to need at least a year to produce the definitive syllabuses. They will wish to consult with subject teachers to ensure that what they are producing is practicable and acceptable. They may need to liaise with publishers if new approaches will require new textbooks. The syllabuses will have to be accompanied by specimen papers, which if at all possible should be produced with as much care as live papers. To teachers the specimen papers are often a better guide to what to expect than the syllabus itself. If after the live examination teachers protest that the specimen papers had turned out to be unhelpful, or even positively misleading, the Board will receive, and deserve, little sympathy if it argues that the specimens had not been produced with full quality controls. Finally, before printing and distribution can begin, the new syllabuses and their accompanying specimen papers will have to be approved by the QCA. It is very unusual for a syllabus to pass this stage unscathed. Those who vet it are almost certain to find some points of detail which can be improved or could be better expressed. Even in the unlikely event of the first draft being perfect, when someone is being paid a substantial fee to vet it he is likely to feel obliged to raise a number of points, if only to convince whoever is paying him that he has done the job properly. This may be a cynical view, but I know that if I paid someone to review a document and received a reply which said that there were no points to make I should wonder whether he had read it. Similarly when I review a document I feel obliged to make a string of comments, although I hope that as many as possible may be complimentary, so that I can prove my conscientiousness without creating problems for anyone else!

This whole process can clearly run to at least two years, and probably three, before a decision to revise can lead to the start of teaching. The first examination will take place two years later, at which point one can make a first judgement on the effectiveness of the reform. If there are clear weaknesses and problems, they cannot be put right quickly. The second batch of students is already halfway through the course; the third batch is entering upon it. A new examination will run for a minimum of three years before anything other than the most marginal of tinkering can be done to change it. How important it is, then, to get it right first time, which means that haste must be avoided at all costs. Any Secretary of State must know that reforms which he initiates will probably bear fruit in the time of the next government, and perhaps under the aegis of the rival party.

Those working to improve our education and examining systems also suffer from the fact that almost everyone else, from the highest government members, through civil servants, especially through journalists, down to the humblest members of the general public, believe that they know what happens in education and what should be done about it. We have all been to school and seen what teachers do; we have all sat examinations and formed our view of how they work. In consequence we all feel entitled to say what is wrong and what should be done. Perhaps much in the pages of this book will have shown readers that the issues are complex at a level that few can appreciate unless they are centrally involved. No one in education fully understands the issues in any subject other than his own. How can non-specialists expect to produce a panacea for the whole system?

To my mind the greatest stumbling block in producing a truly successful system has been that very objective: to produce a system. When a policy is put forward which requires all subjects to have a common pattern, or all candidates to follow a common course, or all examinations to have a common structure, I know that in some areas it will not work. When GCSE was first launched, one of the central slogans was 'Fitness for purpose'. If that were the basic criterion in evaluating all details in the implementation of educational policy, there might be a lack of uniformity, perhaps distressing to some, but I am convinced that there would be real progress.

Index